POETRY FROM CRESCENT MOON

Walking In Cornwall
by Ursula Le Guin

Hymns To the Night
by Novalis

Hymns To the Night: In Translation
by Novalis

Flower Pollen: Selected Thoughts
by Novalis

Novalis: His Life, Thoughts and Works
by Novalis

Edmund Spenser: *Heavenly Love: Selected Poems*
selected and introduced by Teresa Page

Edmund Spenser: *Amoretti*
edited by Teresa Page

The Visions of Petrarch and Bellay: Early Sonnets
by Edmund Spenser

Robert Herrick: *Delight In Disorder: Selected Poems*
edited and introduced by M.K. Pace

Robert Herrick: *Hesperides*
edited and introduced by M.K. Pace

Robert Herrick: *Upon Julia's Breasts: Love Poems*
edited and introduced by M.K. Pace

Sir Thomas Wyatt: *Love For Love: Selected Poems*
selected and introduced by Louise Cooper

John Donne: *Air and Angels: Selected Poems*
selected and introduced by A.H. Ninham

D.H. Lawrence: *Being Alive: Selected Poems*
edited with an introduction by Margaret Elvy

D.H. Lawrence: *Amores*
edited with an introduction by Margaret Elvy

D.H. Lawrence: *Look! We Have Come Through!*
edited with an introduction by Margaret Elvy

D.H. Lawrence: *Love Poems and Others*
edited with an introduction by Margaret Elvy

D.H. Lawrence: *New Poems*
edited with an introduction by Margaret Elvy

D.H. Lawrence: *Symbolic Landscapes*
by Jane Foster

D.H. Lawrence: *Infinite Sensual Violence*
by M.K. Pace

Percy Bysshe Shelley: *Paradise of Golden Lights: Selected Poems*
selected and introduced by Charlotte Greene

Thomas Hardy: *Her Haunting Ground: Selected Poems*
edited, with an introduction by A.H. Ninham

Thomas Hardy: *Late Lyrics and Earlier*
edited, with an introduction by A.H. Ninham

Thomas Hardy: *Moments of Vision*
edited, with an introduction by A.H. Ninham

Thomas Hardy: *Poems of the Past and the Present*
edited, with an introduction by A.H. Ninham

Thomas Hardy: *Satires of Circumstance*
edited, with an introduction by A.H. Ninham

Thomas Hardy: *Time's Laughingstocks*
edited, with an introduction by A.H. Ninham

Thomas Hardy: *Wessex Poems*
edited, with an introduction by A.H. Ninham

Sexing Hardy: Thomas Hardy and Feminism
by Margaret Elvy

Emily Bronte: *Darkness and Glory: Selected Poems*
selected and introduced by Miriam Chalk

John Keats: *Bright Star: Selected Poems*
edited with an introduction by Miriam Chalk

John Keats: *Poems of 1820*
edited with an introduction by Miriam Chalk

Henry Vaughan: *A Great Ring of Pure and Endless Light: Selected Poems*
selected and introduced by A.H. Ninham

The Crescent Moon Book of Love Poetry
edited by Louise Cooper

The Crescent Moon Book of Mystical Poetry in English
edited by Carol Appleby

The Crescent Moon Book of Nature Poetry From Langland to Lawrence
edited by Margaret Elvy

The Crescent Moon Book of Metaphysical Poetry
edited and introduced by Charlotte Greene

The Crescent Moon Book of Elizabethan Love Poetry
edited and introduced by Carol Appleby

The Crescent Moon Book of Romantic Poetry
edited and introduced by L.M. Poole

Brigitte's Blue Heart
by Jeremy Reed

Claudia Schiffer's Red Shoes
by Jeremy Reed

By-Blows: Uncollected Poems
by D.J. Enright

Peter Redgrove: Here Comes the Flood
by Jeremy Mark Robinson

Sex-Magic-Poetry-Cornwall: A Flood of Poems
by Peter Redgrove, edited with an essay by Jeremy Mark Robinson

The Troubadours
by H.J. Chaytor

Petrarch, Dante and the Troubadours: The Religion of Love and Poetry
by Cassidy Hughes

Fifteen Sonnets of Petrarch
by Francesco Petrarch
Canzoniere
by Francesco Petrarch

Dante: *Selections From the Vita Nuova*
translated by Thomas Okey

Dante: *Vita Nuova*
translated by Dante Gabriel Rossetti

Dante: *De Monarchia*
translated by F.J. Church

Dante: His Times and His Work
by Arthur John Butler

Arthur Rimbaud: *Selected Poems*
edited and translated by Andrew Jary

Arthur Rimbaud: *A Season in Hell*
edited and translated by Andrew Jary

Friedrich Hölderlin: *Hölderlin's Songs of Light: Selected Poems*
translated by Michael Hamburger

Rainer Maria Rilke: *Dance the Orange: Selected Poems*
translated by Michael Hamburger

Rainer Maria Rilke: *Poems*
translated by Jessie Lamont

Auguste Rodin
by Rainer Maria Rilke

Rilke: Space, Essence and Angels In the Poetry of Rainer Maria Rilke
by B.D. Barnacle

German Romantic Poetry: Goethe, Novalis, Heine, Hölderlin
by Carol Appleby

The North Sea
by Heinrich Heine

Rampoli: Poems From Mainly German
by George Macdonald

Arseny Tarkovsky: *Life, Life: Selected Poems*
translated by Virginia Rounding

Emily Dickinson: *Wild Nights: Selected Poems*
selected and introduced by Miriam Chalk

Diana
by Henry Constable

Delia
by Samuel Daniel

Idea
by Michael Drayton

Astrophil and Stella
by Sir Philip Sidney

Selected Poems
by William Shakespeare

Elizabethan Sonnet Cycles
by Daniel, Drayton, Sidney,
Spenser and Shakespeare

Elizabethan Sonnet Cycles (Volume Two)
by Lodge, Griffin, Smith,
Constable and Fletcher

Three Metaphysical Poets
edited by A.H. Ninham

Three Romantic Poets
edited by Miriam Chalk

CHARLES BAUDELAIRE

THE POEMS AND PROSE POEMS

CHARLES BAUDELAIRE

THE POEMS AND PROSE POEMS

INTRODUCTION BY JAMES HUNEKER

TRANSLATD BY JAMES HUNEKER

EDITED BY JEREMY MARK ROBINSON

WITH THE FRENCH TEXT

CRESCENT MOON

First published 1919. This edition © 2024.

Set in Book Antiqua 10 on 14pt.
Designed by Radiance Graphics.

All rights reserved. No part of this book may be reprinted or reproduced, stored in a retrieval system, or transmitted, in any form or by any means, electronic, mechanical, photocopying, recording or otherwise, without permission from the publisher.

Images are used for information and research purposes, with no infringement of copyright or rights intended.

Thanks to the authors and publishers quoted.

British Library Cataloguing in Publication data

ISBN-13 9781861718167
ISBN-13 9781861719027

CRESCENT MOON PUBLISHING
P.O. Box 1312, Maidstone, Kent, ME14 5XU
Great Britain, www.crmoon.com

CONTENTS

Note On the Text ❊ 13

CHARLES BAUDELAIRE by James Huneker ❊ 19

THE FLOWERS OF EVIL

The Dance of Death ❊ 56
The Beacons ❊ 62
The Sadness of the Moon ❊ 66
Exotic Perfume ❊ 68
Beauty ❊ 70
The Balcony ❊ 72
The Sick Muse ❊ 76
The Venal Muse ❊ 78
The Evil Monk ❊ 80
The Temptation ❊ 82
The Irreparable ❊ 84
A Former Life ❊ 88
Don Juan in Hades ❊ 90
The Living Flame ❊ 92
Correspondences ❊ 94
The Flask ❊ 96
Reversibility ❊ 99
The Eyes of Beauty ❊ 101
Sonnet of Autumn ❊ 103
The Remorse of the Dead ❊ 105
The Ghost ❊ 107
To a Madonna ❊ 109

The Sky ❋ 113
Spleen ❋ 115
The Owls ❋ 117
Bien Loin D'Ici ❋ 119
Music ❋ 121
Contemplation ❋ 123
To a Brown Beggar-maid ❋ 125
The Swan ❋ 131
The Seven Old Men ❋ 136
The Little Old Women ❋ 140
A Madrigal of Sorrow ❋ 147
The Ideal ❋ 151
Mist and Rain ❋ 153
Sunset ❋ 155
The Corpse ❋ 157
An Allegory ❋ 161
The Accursed ❋ 163
La Beatrice ❋ 167
The Soul of Wine ❋ 169
The Wine of Lovers ❋ 171
The Death of Lovers ❋ 173
The Death of The Poor ❋ 175
The Benediction ❋ 177
Gypsies Travelling ❋ 183
Franciscæ Meæ Laudes ❋ 185
Robed in a Silken Robe ❋ 189
A Landscape ❋ 191
The Voyage ❋ 194

LITTLE POEMS IN PROSE

The Stranger ❋ 208
Every Man His Chimæra ❋ 210
Venus and the Fool ❋ 212
Intoxication ❋ 214
The Gifts of the Moon ❋ 216
The Invitation to the Voyage ❋ 218

What Is Truth? ❋ 224
Already! ❋ 226
The Double Chamber ❋ 230
At One O'clock in the Morning ❋ 236
The Confiteor of the Artist ❋ 240
The Thyrsus ❋ 242
The Marksman ❋ 246
The Shooting-range and the Cemetery ❋ 248
The Desire to Paint ❋ 250
The Glass-Vendor ❋ 252
The Widows ❋ 258
The Temptations; or, Eros, Plutus, and Glory ❋ 264

A Note On Charles Baudelaire ❋ 272

NOTE ON THE TEXT

The text is from *The Poems and Prose Poems* by Charles Baudelaire, published by Brentano's, New York, in 1919.

"Close to your hand lies a little volume, bound in some Nile-green skin that has been pounded with gilded nenuphars, and smoothed with hard ivory. It is the book that Gautier loved, it is Baudelaire's masterpiece."

OSCAR WILDE ("Intentions").

Charles Baudelaire by Felix Nadar, 1855.

Charles Baudelaire by Gustave Courbet, 1849

CHARLES BAUDELAIRE

BY JAMES HUNEKER

I

For the sentimental no greater foe exists than the iconoclast who dissipates literary legends. And he is abroad nowadays. Those golden times when they gossiped of De Quincey's enormous opium consumption, of the gin absorbed by gentle Charles Lamb, of Coleridge's dark ways, Byron's escapades, and Shelley's atheism – alas! into what faded limbo have they vanished. Poe, too, whom we saw in fancy reeling from Richmond to Baltimore, Baltimore to Philadelphia, Philadelphia to New York. Those familiar fascinating anecdotes have gone the way of all such jerry-built spooks. We now know Poe to have been a man suffering at the time of his death from cerebral lesion, a man who drank at intervals and little. Dr. Guerrier of Paris has exploded a darling superstition about De Quincey's opium-eating. He has demonstrated that no man could have lived so long – De Quincey was nearly seventy-five at his death – and worked so hard, if he had consumed twelve thousand drops of laudanum as often as he said he did. Furthermore, the English essayist's description of the drug's effects is inexact. He was seldom sleepy – a sure sign, asserts Dr. Guerrier, that he was not altogether enslaved by the drug habit. Sprightly in old age, his powers of labour were prolonged until past three-score and ten. His imagination needed little opium to produce the famous Confessions. Even Gautier's revolutionary red waistcoat worn at the première of Hernani was, according to Gautier, a pink doublet. And Rousseau has been whitewashed. So they are disappearing, those literary legends, until, disheartened, we cry out: Spare us our dear, old-fashioned, disreputable men of genius!

But the legend of Charles Baudelaire is seemingly indestructible. This French poet has suffered more from the friendly malignant biographer and chroniclers than did Poe. Who shall keep the curs out of the cemetery? asked Baudelaire after he had read Griswold on Poe. A few years later his own cemetery was invaded and the world was put into possession of the Baudelaire legend; that legend of the atrabilious, irritable poet, dandy, maniac, his hair dyed green, spouting blasphemies; that grim, despairing image of a diabolic, a libertine, saint, and drunkard. Maxime du Camp was much to blame for the promulgation of these tales – witness his Souvenirs littéraires. However, it may be confessed that part of the Baudelaire legend was created by Charles Baudelaire. In the history of literature it is difficult to parallel such a deliberate piece of self-stultification. Not Villon, who preceded him, not Verlaine, who imitated him, drew for the astonishment or disedification of the world a like unflattering portrait. Mystifier as he was, he must have suffered at times from acute cortical irritation. And, notwithstanding his desperate effort to realize Poe's idea, he only proved Poe correct, who had said that no man can bare his heart quite naked; there always will be something held back, something false ostentatiously thrust forward. The grimace, the attitude, the pomp of rhetoric are so many buffers between the soul of man and the sharp reality of published confessions. Baudelaire was no more exception to this rule than St. Augustine, Bunyan, Rousseau, or Huysmans; though he was as frank as any of them, as we may see in the printed diary, Mon cœur mis à nu (Posthumous Works, Société du Mercure de France); and in the Journal, Fusées, Letters, and other fragments exhumed by devoted Baudelarians.

To smash legends, Eugène Crépet's biographical study, first printed in 1887, has been republished with new notes by his son,

Jacques Crépet. This is an exceedingly valuable contribution to Baudelaire lore; a dispassionate life, however, has yet to be written, a noble task for some young poet who will disentangle the conflicting lies originated by Baudelaire – that tragic comedian – from the truth and thus save him from himself. The Crépet volume is really but a series of notes; there are some letters addressed to the poet by the distinguished men of his day, supplementing the rather disappointing volume of Letters, 1841-1866, published in 1908. There are also documents in the legal prosecution of Baudelaire, with memories of him by Charles Asselineau, Léon Cladel, Camille Lemonnier, and others.

In November, 1850, Maxime du Camp and Gustave Flaubert found themselves at the French Ambassador's, Constantinople. The two friends had taken a trip in the Orient which later bore fruit in Salammbô. General Aupick, the representative of the French Government, cordially the young men received; they were presented to his wife, Madame Aupick. She was the mother of Charles Baudelaire, and inquired rather anxiously of Du Camp: "My son has talent, has he not?" Unhappy because her second marriage, a brilliant one, had set her son against her, the poor woman welcomed from such a source confirmation of her eccentric boy's gifts. Du Camp tells the much-discussed story of a quarrel between the youthful Charles and his stepfather, a quarrel that began at table. There were guests present. After some words Charles bounded at the General's throat and sought to strangle him. He was promptly boxed on the ears and succumbed to a nervous spasm. A delightful anecdote, one that fills with joy psychiatrists in search of a theory of genius and degeneration. Charles was given some money and put on board a ship sailing to East India. He became a cattle-dealer in the British army, and returned to France years afterward with a Vénus noire, to whom he addressed extravagant poems! All this according to Du Camp. Here is another tale, a comical one. Baudelaire visited Du Camp in Paris, and his hair was violently green. Du Camp said nothing. Angered by this indifference, Baudelaire asked: "You find nothing abnormal about me?" "No," was the answer. "But my hair – it is green!" "That is not singular, mon cher Baudelaire; every one has hair more or less green in Paris." Disappointed in not creating a sensation, Baudelaire went to a café, gulped down two large bottles of Burgundy, and asked the waiter to remove the water, as water was a disagreeable sight; then he went away in a rage. It is a pity to doubt this green hair legend; presently a man of genius will not be able to enjoy an epileptic fit in peace – as does a banker or a beggar. We are told that St. Paul, Mahomet, Handel, Napoleon, Flaubert, Dostoiëvsky were epileptoids; yet we do not encounter men of this rare kind among the inmates of asylums. Even Baudelaire had his sane moments.

The joke of the green hair has been disposed of by Crépet. Baudelaire's hair thinning after an illness, he had his head shaved and painted with salve of a green hue, hoping thereby to escape baldness. At the time when he had embarked for Calcutta (May, 1841), he was not seventeen, but twenty years of age. Du Camp said he was seventeen when he attacked General Aupick. The dinner could not have taken place at Lyons because the Aupick family had left that city six years before the date given by Du Camp. Charles was provided with five thousand francs for his expenses, instead of twenty – Du Camp's version – and he never was a beef-drover in the British army, for a good reason – he never reached India. Instead, he disembarked at the Isle of Bourbon, and after a short stay suffered from homesickness and returned to France, after being absent about ten months. But, like Flaubert, on his return home Baudelaire was seized with the nostalgia of the East; over there he had yearned for Paris. Jules Claretie recalls Baudelaire saying to him with a grimace: "I love Wagner; but the music I prefer is that of a cat hung up by his tail outside of a window, and trying to stick to the panes of glass with its claws. There is an odd grating on the glass which I find at the same time strange, irritating, and singularly harmonious." Is it necessary to add that Baudelaire, notorious in Paris for his love of cats, dedicating poems to cats, would never have perpetrated such revolting cruelty?

Another misconception, a critical one, is the case of Poe and Baudelaire. The young Frenchman first became infatuated with Poe's writings in 1846 or 1847 – he gave these two dates, though several stories of Poe had been translated into French as early as 1841 or 1842; L'Orang-Outang was the first, which we know as The Murders in the Rue Morgue; Madame Meunier also adapted several Poe stories for the reviews. Baudelaire's labours as a translator lasted over ten years. That he assimilated Poe, that he idolized Poe, is a commonplace of literary gossip. But that Poe had overwhelming influence in the formation of his poetic genius is not the truth. Yet we find such an acute critic as the late Edmund Clarence Stedman writing, "Poe's chief influence upon Baudelaire's own production relates to poetry." It is precisely the reverse. Poe's influence affected Baudelaire's prose, notably in the disjointed confessions, Mon cœur mis à nu, which vaguely recall the American writer's Marginalia. The bulk in the poetry in Les Fleurs du Mal was written before Baudelaire had read Poe, though not published in book form until 1857. But in 1855 some of the poems saw the light in the Revue des deux Mondes, while many of them had been put forth a decade or fifteen years before as fugitive verse in various magazines. Stedman was not the first to make this mistake. In Bayard Taylor's The Echo Club we find on page 24 this criticism: "There was a congenital twist about Poe ... Baudelaire and Swinburne after him have been trying to surpass him by increasing the dose; but his muse is the natural Pythia inheriting her convulsions, while they eat all sorts of insane roots to produce theirs." This must have been written about 1872, and after reading it one would fancy that Poe and Baudelaire were rhapsodic wrigglers on the poetic tripod, whereas their poetry is often reserved, even glacial. Baudelaire, like Poe, sometimes "built his nests with the birds of Night," and that was enough to condemn the work of both men by critics of the didactic school.

Once, when Baudelaire heard that an American man of

letters(?) was in Paris, he secured an introduction and called on him. Eagerly inquiring after Poe, he learned that he was not considered a genteel person in America, Baudelaire withdrew, muttering maledictions. Enthusiastic poet! Charming literary person! Yet the American, whoever he was, represented public opinion at the time. To-day criticisms of Poe are vitiated by the desire to make him an angel. It is to be doubted whether without his barren environment and hard fortunes we should have had Poe at all. He had to dig down deep into the pit of his personality to reach the central core of his music. But every ardent young soul entering "literature" begins by a vindication of Poe's character. Poe was a man, and he is now a classic. He was a half-charlatan as was Baudelaire. In both the sublime and the sickly were never far asunder. The pair loved to mystify, to play pranks on their contemporaries. Both were implacable pessimists. Both were educated in affluence, and both had to face unprepared the hardships of life. The hastiest comparison of their poetic work will show that their only common ideal was the worship of an exotic beauty. Their artistic methods of expression were totally dissimilar. Baudelaire, like Poe, had a harp-like temperament which vibrated in the presence of strange subjects. Above all, he was obsessed by sex. Women, as angel of destruction, is the keynote of his poems. Poe was almost sexless. His aerial creatures never footed the dusty highways of the world. His lovely lines, "Helen, thy beauty is to me," could never have been written by Baudelaire; while Poe would never have pardoned the "fulgurant" grandeur, the Beethoven-like harmonies, the Dantesque horrors of that "deep wide music of lost souls" in "Femmes Damnées":

"Descendes, descendes, lamentable victimes."

Or this, which might serve as a text for one of John Martin's vast sinister mezzotints:

> J'ai vu parfois au fond d'un théâtre banal
> Qu'enflammait l'orchestre sonore,
> Une fée allumer dans un ciel infernal
> Une miraculeuse aurore;
>
> J'ai vu parfois au fond d'un théâtre banal
> Un être, qui n'était que lumière, or et gaze,
> Terrasser rénorme Satan;
> Mais mon cœur que jamais ne visite l'extase,
> Est un théâtre où l'on attend
> Toujours, toujours en vain l'Etre aux ailes de gaze.

George Saintsbury thus sums up the differences between Poe and Baudelaire: "Both authors – Poe and De Quincey – fell short of Baudelaire himself as regards depth and fulness of passion, but both have a superficial likeness to him in eccentricity of temperameut and affection for a certain peculiar mixture of grotesque and horror." Poe is without passion, except a passion for the macabre; what Huysmans calls "The October of the sensations"; whereas, there is a gulf of despair and terror and humanity in Baudelaire, which shakes your nerves, yet stimulates the imagination. However, profounder as a poet, he was no match for Poe in what might be termed intellectual prestidigitation. The mathematical Poe, the Poe of the ingenious detective tales, tales extraordinary, the Poe of the swift flights into the cosmic blue, the Poe the prophet and mystic – in these the American was more versatile than his French translator. That Baudelaire said, "Evil be thou my good," is doubtless true. He proved all things and found them vanity. He is the poet of original sin, a worshipper of Satan for the sake of paradox; his Litanies to Satan ring childish to us – in his heart he was a believer. His was "an infinite reverse aspiration," and mixed up with his pose was a disgust for vice, for life itself. He was the last of the Romanticists; Sainte-Beuve called him the Kamchatka of Romanticism; its remotest hyperborean peak. Romanticism is dead to-day, as dead as Naturalism; but Baudelaire is alive, and read. His glistening phosphorescent trail is over French poetry and he is the begetter of a school: –

Verlaine, Villiers de l'Isle Adam, Carducci, Arthur Rimbaud, Jules Laforgue, Gabriel D'Annunzio, Aubrey Beardsley, Verhaeren, and many of the youthful crew. He affected Swinburne, and in Huysmans, who was not a poet, his splenetic spirit lives. Baudelaire's motto might be the obverse of Browning's lines: "The Devil is in heaven. All's wrong with the world."

When Goethe said of Hugo and the Romanticists that they came from Chateaubriand, he should have substituted the name of Rousseau – "Romanticism, it is Rousseau," exclaims Pierre Lasserre. But there is more of Byron and Petrus Borel – a forgotten half-mad poet – in Baudelaire; though, for a brief period, in 1848, he became a Rousseau reactionary, sported the workingman's blouse, cut his hair, shouldered a musket, went to the barricades, wrote inflammatory editorials calling the proletarian "Brother!" (oh, Baudelaire!) and, as the Goncourts recorded in their diary, had the head of a maniac. How seriously we may take this swing of the pendulum is to be noted in a speech of the poet's at the time of the Revolution: "Come," he said, "let us go shoot General Aupick!" It was his stepfather that he thought of, not the eternal principles of Liberty. This may be a false anecdote; many such were foisted upon Baudelaire. For example, his exclamations at cafés or in public places, such as: "Have you ever eaten a baby? I find it pleasing to the palate!" or, "The night I killed my father!" Naturally, people stared and Baudelaire was happy – he had startled a bourgeois. The cannibalistic idea he may have borrowed from Swift's amusing pamphlet, for this French poet knew English literature.

Gautier compares the poems to a certain tale of Hawthorne's in which there is a garden of poisoned flowers. But Hawthorne worked in his laboratory of evil wearing mask and gloves; he never descended into the mud and sin of the street. Baudelaire ruined his health, smudged his soul, yet remained withal, as Anatole France says, "a divine poet." How childish, yet how touching is his resolution – he wrote in his diary of prayer's dynamic force – when he was penniless, in debt, threatened with imprisonment, sick, nauseated with sin: "To make every morning my prayer to God, the reservoir of all force, and all justice; to my father, to Mariette, and to Poe as intercessors." (Evidently, Maurice Barrès encountered here his theory of Intercessors.) Baudelaire loved the memory of his father as much as Stendhal hated his own. He became reconciled with his mother after the death of General Aupick, in 1857. He felt in 1862 that his own intellectual eclipse was approaching, for he wrote: "I have cultivated my hysteria with joy and terror. To-day imbecility's wing fanned me as it passed." The sense of the vertiginous gulf was abiding with him; read his poem, "Pascal avait son gouffre."

In preferring the Baudelaire translations of Poe to the original – and they give the impression of being original works – Stedman agreed with Asselineau that the French is more concise than the English. The prose of Poe and Baudelaire is clear, sober, rhythmic; Baudelaire's is more lapidary, finer in contour, richer coloured, more supple, though without the "honey and tiger's blood" of Barbey d'Aurevilly. Baudelaire's soul was patiently built up as a fabulous bird might build its nest – bits of straw, the sobbing of women, clay, cascades of black stars, rags, leaves, rotten wood, corroding dreams, a spray of roses, a sparkle of pebble, a gleam of blue sky, arabesques of incense and verdigris, despairing hearts and music and the abomination of desolation, for its ground-tones. But this soul-nest is also a cemetery of the seven sorrows. He loves the clouds ... les nuages ... là bas.... It was là bas with him even in the tortures of his wretched love-life. Corruption and death were ever floating in his consciousness. He was like Flaubert, who saw everywhere the hidden skeleton. Félicien Hops has best interpreted Baudelaire; the etcher and poet were closely knit spirits. Rodin, too, is a Baudelarian. If there could be such an anomaly as a native wood-note wildly evil, it would be the lyric and astringent voice of this poet. His sensibility was both catholic and morbid, though he could be frigid in the face of the most disconcerting misfortunes. He was a man for whom the invisible word existed; if Gautier was pagan,

Baudelaire was a strayed spirit from mediæval days. The spirit rules, and, as Paul Bourget said, "he saw God." A Manichean in his worship of evil, he nevertheless abased his soul: "Oh! Lord God! Give me the force and courage to contemplate my heart and my body without disgust," he prays: but as some one remarked to Rochefoucauld, "Where you end, Christianity begins."

Baudelaire built his ivory tower on the borders of a poetic Maremma, which every miasma of the spirit pervaded, every marsh-light and glow-worm inhabited. Like Wagner, Baudelaire painted in his sultry music the profundities of abysms, the vastness of space. He painted, too, the great nocturnal silences of the soul.

Pacem summum tenent! He never reached peace on the heights. Let us admit that souls of his kind are encased in sick frames; their steel is too shrewd for the scabbard; yet the enigma for us is none the less unfathomable. Existence for such natures is a sort of muffled delirium. To affiliate him with Poe, De Quincey, Hoffman, James Thomson, Coleridge, and the rest of the sombre choir does not explain him; he is, perhaps, nearer Donne and Villon than any of the others – strains of the metaphysical and sinister and supersubtle are to be discovered in him. The disharmony of brain and body, the spiritual bilocation, are only too easy to diagnose; but the remedy? Hypocrite lecteur – mon semblable – mon frère! When the subtlety, force, grandeur, of his poetic production be considered, together with its disquieting, nervous, vibrating qualities, it is not surprising that Victor Hugo wrote to the poet: "You invest the heaven of art with we know not what deadly rays; you create a new shudder." Hugo might have said that he turned Art into an Inferno. Baudelaire is the evil archangel of poetry. In his heaven of fire, glass and ebony he is the blazing Lucifer. "A glorious devil, large in heart and brain, that did love beauty only..." once sang Tennyson, though not of the Frenchman.

II

As long ago as 1869, and in our "barbarous gas-lit country," as Baudelaire named the land of Poe, an unsigned review appeared in which this poet was described as "unique and as interesting as Hamlet. He is that rare and unknown being, a genuine poet – a poet in the midst of things that have disordered his spirit – a poet excessively developed in his taste for and by beauty ... very responsive to the ideal, very greedy of sensation." A better description of Baudelaire does not exist The Hamlet-motive, particularly, is one that sounded throughout the disordered symphony of the poet's life.

He was, later, revealed – also reviled – to American readers by Henry James, who completely missed his significance. This was in 1878, when appeared the first edition of French Poets and Novelists. Previous to that there had been some desultory discussion, a few essays in the magazines, and in 1875 a sympathetic paper by Professor James Albert Harrison of the University of Virginia. He denounced the Frenchman for his reprehensible taste, though he did not mention his beautiful verse nor his originality in the matter of criticism. Baudelaire, in his eyes, was not only immoral, but he had, with the approbation of Sainte-Beuve, introduced Poe as a great man to the French nation. (See Baudelaire's letter to Sainte-Beuve in the newly published Letters, 1841-1866.) Perhaps "Mr. Dick Minim" and his projected

Academy of Criticism might make clear these devious problems.

The Etudes Critiques of Edmond Schérer were collected in 1863. In them we find this unhappy, uncritical judgment: "Baudelaire, lui, n'a rien, ni le cœur, ni l'esprit, ni l'idée, ni le mot, ni la raison, ni la fantaisie, ni la verve, ni même la facture ... son unique titre c'est d'avoir contribué à créer l'esthétique de la débauche." It is not our intention to dilate upon the injustice of this criticism. It is Baudelaire the critic of æsthetics in whom we are interested. Yet I cannot forbear saying that if all the negations of Schérer had been transformed into affirmations, only justice would have been accorded Baudelaire, who was not alone a poet, the most original of his century, but also a critic of the first rank, one who welcomed Richard Wagner when Paris hooted him and his fellow composer, Hector Berlioz, played the rôle of the envious; one who fought for Edouard Manet, Leconte de Lisle, Gustave Flaubert, Eugène Delacroix; fought with pen for the modern etchers, illustrators, Meryon, Daumier, Félicien Rops, Gavarni, and Constantin Guys. He literally identified himself with De Quincey and Poe, translating them so wonderfully well that some unpatriotic persons like the French better than the originals. So much was Baudelaire absorbed in Poe that a writer of his times asserted that the translator would meet the same fate as the American poet. A singular, vigorous spirit is Baudelaire's, whose poetry with its "icy ecstasy" is profound and harmonious, whose criticism is penetrated by a catholic quality, who anticipated modern critics in his abhorrence of schools and environments, preferring to isolate the man and uniquely study him. He would have subscribed to Swinburne's generous pronouncement: "I have never been able to see what should attract man to the profession of criticism but the noble pleasure of praising." The Frenchman has said that it would be impossible for a critic to become a poet; and it is impossible for a poet not to contain a critic.

Théophile Gautier's study prefixed to the definitive edition of Les Fleurs du Mal is not only the most sympathetic exposition of

Baudelaire as man and genius, but it is also the high-water mark of Gautier's gifts as a critical essayist. We learn therein how the young Charles, an incorrigible dandy, came to visit Hôtel Pimodan about 1844. In this Hôtel Pimodan a dilettante, Ferdinand Boissard, held high revel. His fantastically decorated apartments were frequented by the painters, poets, sculptors, romancers, of the day – that is, carefully selected ones such as Liszt, George Sand, Mérimée, and others whose verve or genius gave them the privilege of saying Open Sesame! to this cave of forty Supermen. Balzac has in his Peau de Chagrin pictured the same sort of scenes which were supposed to occur weekly at the Pimodan. Gautier eloquently describes the meeting of these kindred artistic souls, where the beautiful Jewess, Maryx, who had posed for Ary Scheffer's Mignon and for Paul Delaroche's La Gloire, met the superb Madame Sabatier, the only woman that Baudelaire loved, and the original of that extraordinary group of Clésinger's – the sculptor and son-in-law of George Sand – la Femme au Serpent, a Salammbô à la mode in marble. Hasheesh was eaten, so Gautier writes, by Boissard and Baudelaire. As for the creator of Mademoiselle Maupin, he was too robust for such nonsense. He had to work for his living at journalism, and he died in harness, an irreproachable father, while the unhappy Baudelaire, the inheritor of an intense, unstable temperament, soon devoured his patrimony of 75,000 francs, and for the remaining years of his life was between the devil of his dusky Jenny Duval and the deep sea of hopeless debt.

It was at these Pimodan gatherings, which were no doubt much less wicked than the participants would have us believe, that Baudelaire encountered Emile Deroy, a painter of skill, who made his portrait, and encouraged the fashionable young fellow to continue his art studies. We have seen an album containing sketches by the poet. They betray talent of about the same order as Thackeray's, with a superadded note of the "horrific" – that favourite epithet of the early Poe critics. Baudelaire admired Thackeray, and when the Englishman praised the illustrations of

Guys, he was delighted. Deroy taught his pupil the commonplaces of a painter's technique; also how to compose a palette – a rather meaningless phrase nowadays. At least, he did not write of the arts without some technical experience. Delacroix took up his enthusiastic disciple, and when the Salons of Baudelaire appeared in 1845, 1846, 1855, and 1859, the praise and blame they evoked were testimonies to the training and knowledge of their author. A new spirit had been born.

The names of Diderot and Baudelaire were coupled. Neither academic nor spouting the jargon of the usual critic, the Salons of Baudelaire are the production of a humanist. Some would put them above Diderot's. Mr. Saintsbury, after Swinburne the warmest advocate of Baudelaire among the English, thinks that the French poet in his picture criticism observed too little and imagined too much. "In other words," he adds, "to read a criticism of Baudelaire's without the title affixed is by no means a sure method of recognizing the picture afterward." Now, word-painting was the very thing that Baudelaire avoided. It was his friend Gautier, with the plastic style, who attempted the well-nigh impossible feat of competing in his verbal descriptions with the certitudes of canvas and marble. And, if he with his verbal imagination did not entirely succeed, how could a less adept manipulator of the vocabulary? We do not agree with Mr. Saintsbury. No one can imagine too much when the imagination is that of a poet. Baudelaire divined the work of the artist and set it down scrupulously in a prose of exceeding rectitude. He did not paint pictures in prose. He did not divagate. He did not overburden his pages with technical terms. But the spirit of his subject he did disengage in a few swift phrases. The polemics of historical schools were a cross for him to bear, and he wore his prejudices lightly. Like a true critic, he judged more by form than theme. There are no types; there is only life, he asserted, and long before Jules Laforgue. He was ever art-for-art, yet, having breadth of comprehension and a Heine-like capacity for seeing both sides of his own nature with its idiosyncrasies, he could write: "The puerile utopia of the school of art-for-art, in excluding morality, and often even passion, was necessarily sterile. All literature which refuses to advance fraternally between science and philosophy is a homicidal and a suicidal literature."

Baudelaire, then, was no less sound a critic of the plastic arts than of music and literature. Like his friend Flaubert, he had a horror of democracy, of the democratisation of the arts, of all the sentimental fuss and fuddle of a pseudo-humanitarianism. During the 1848 agitation the former dandy of 1840 put on a blouse and spoke of barricades. Those things were in the air. Wagner rang the alarm-bells during the Dresden uprising. Chopin wrote for the pianoforte a revolutionary étude. Brave lads! Poets and musicians fight their battles best in the region of the ideal. Baudelaire's little attack of the equality-measles soon vanished. He lectured his brother poets and artists on the folly and injustice of abusing or despising the bourgeois (being a man of paradox, he dedicated a volume of his Salons to the bourgeois), but he would not have contradicted Mr. George Moore for declaring that "in art the democrat is always reactionary. In 1830 the democrats were against Victor Hugo and Delacrois." And Les Fleurs du Mal, that book of opals, blood, and evil swamp-flowers, will never be savoured by the mob.

In his Souvenirs de Jeunesse, Champfleury speaks of the promenades in the Louvre he enjoyed the company with Baudelaire. Bronzino was one of the poet's preferences. He was also attracted by El Greco – not an unnatural admiration, considering the sombre extravagance of his own genius. Of Goya he has written in exalted phrases. Velasquez was his touchstone. Being of a perverse nature, his Derves ruined by abuse of drink and drugs, the landscapes of his imagination were more beautiful than Nature herself. The country itself, he declared, was odious. Like Whistler, whom he often met – see the Hommage à Delacrois by Fantin-Latour, with its portraits of Whistler, Baudelaire, Manet, Bracquemond the etcher, Legros, Delacrois, Cordier, Duranty the critic, and De Balleroy – he could not help showing his aversion to "foolish sunsets." In a word, Baudelaire, into whose brain had entered too much moonlight, was the father of a lunar school of poetry, criticism and fiction. His Samuel Cramer, in La Fanfarlo, is the literary progenitor of Jean, Duc d'Esseintes, in Huysmans's *A Rebours*. Huysmans at first modelled himself upon Baudelaire. His Le Drageoir aux Epices is a continuation of Petits Poèmes en Prose. And to Baudelaire's account must be laid much artificial morbid writing. Despite his pursuit of perfection in form, his influence has been too often baneful to impressionable artists in embryo. A lover of Gallic Byronism, and high-priest of the Satanic school, there was no extravagance, absurd or terrible, that he did not commit, from etching a four-part fugue on ice to skating hymns in honour of Lucifer. In his criticism alone was he the sane logical Frenchman. And while he did not live to see the success of the Impressionist group, he surely would have acclaimed their theory and practice. Was he not an impressionist himself?

As Richard Wagner was his god in music, so Delacroix quite overflowed his æsthetic consciousness. Read Volume II of his collected works, *Curiosités Esthétiques*, which contains his Salons; also his essay, *De l'Essence du Rire* (worthy to be placed side by side with George Meredith's essay on Comedy). Caricaturists, French and foreign, are considered in two chapters at the close of the volume. Baudelaire was as conscientious as Gautier. He trotted around miles of mediocre canvas, saying an encouraging word to the less talented, boiling over with holy indignation or indulging in glacial irony, before the rash usurpers occupying the seats of the mighty, and pouncing on new genius with promptitude. Upon Delacroix he lavished the largesse of his admiration. He smiled at the platitudes of Horace Vernet, and only shook his head over the Schnetzes and other artisans of the day. He welcomed William Hausollier, now so little known. He praised Devéria, Chasseriau – who waited years before he came into his own; his preferred landscapists were Corot, Rousseau and Troyon. He impolitely spoke of Ary Scheffer and the "apes of sentiment"; while his discussions of Hogarth, Cruikshank, Pinelli and

Breughel proclaims his versatility of vision. In his essay Le Peintre de la Vie Moderne he was the first among critics to recognize the peculiar quality called "modernity," that naked vibration which informs the novels of Goncourt, Flaubert's L'Education Sentimentale, and the pictures of Manet, Monet, Degas and Raffaelli with their evocations of a new, nervous Paris. It is in his Volume III, entitled L'Art Romantique, that so many things dear to the new century were then subjects of furious quarrels. This book contains much just and brilliant writing. It was easy for Nietzsche to praise Wagner in Germany in 1876, but dangerous at Paris in 1861 to declare war on Wagner's adverse critics. This Baudelaire did.

The relations of Baudelaire and Edouard Manet were exceedingly cordial. In a letter to Théophile Thoré, the art critic (Letters, p. 361), we find Baudelaire defending his friend from the accusation that his pictures were pastiches of Goya. He wrote: "Manet has never seen Goya, never El Greco; he was never in the Pourtalés Gallery." Which may have been true at the time, 1864, nevertheless Manet had visited Madrid and spent much time studying Velasquez and abusing Spanish cookery. (Consider, too, Goya's Balcony with Girls and Manet's famous Balcony.) Raging at the charge of imitation, Baudelaire said in this same epistle: "They accuse even me of imitating Edgar Poe.... Do you know why I so patiently translated Poe? Because he resembled me." The poet italicized these words. With stupefaction, therefore, he admired the mysterious coincidences of Manet's work with that of Goya and El Greco.

He took Manet seriously. He wrote to him in a paternal and severe tone. Recall his reproof when urging the painter to exhibit his work. "You complain about attacks, but are you the first to endure them? Have you more genius than Chateaubriand and Wagner? They were not killed by derision. And in order not to make you too proud I must tell you that they are models, each in his way, and in a very rich world, while you are only the first in the decrepitude of your art." (Letters, p. 436.)

Would Baudelaire recall these prophetic words if he were able to revisit the glimpses of the Champs Elysées at the Autumn Salons? What would he think of Cézanne? Odilon Redon he would understand, for he is the transposer of Baudelairianism to terms of design and colour. And perhaps the poet whose verse is saturated with tropical hues – he, when young, sailed in southern seas – might appreciate the monstrous debauch of form and colour in the Tahitian canvases of Paul Gauguin.

Baudelaire's preoccupation with pictorial themes may be noted in his verse. He is par excellence the poet of æsthetics. To Daumier he inscribed a poem; and to the sculptor Ernest Christophe, to Delacroix (Sur Tasse en Prison), to Manet, to Guys (Rêve Parisien), to an unknown master (Une Martyre); and Watteau, a Watteau à rebours, is seen in Un Voyage à Cythère; while in Les Phares this poet of the ideal, spleen music, and perfume, shows his adoration for Rubens, Leonardo da Vinci, Michelangelo, Rembrandt, Puget, Goya, Delacroix – "Delacroix, lac de sang hanté des mauvais anges." And what is more exquisite than his quatrain to Lola de Valence, a poetic inscription for the picture of Edouard Manet, with its last line as vaporous, as subtle as Verlaine: "Le charme inattendu d'un bijou rose et noir!" Heine called himself the last of the Romantics. The first of the "Moderns" and the last of the Romantics was the many-sided Charles Baudelaire.

III

He was born at Paris, April 9, 1821 (Flaubert's birth year), and not April 21, as Gautier has it. His father was Joseph Francis Baudelaire, or Baudelaire, who occupied a government position. A cultivated art lover, his taste was apparent in the home he made for his second wife, Caroline Archimbaut-Dufays, an orphan and the daughter of a military officer. There was a considerable difference in the years of this pair; the mother was twenty-seven, the father sixty-two, at the birth of their only child. By his first marriage the elder Baudelaire had one son, Claude, who, like his half-brother Charles, died of paralysis, though a steady man of business. That great modern neurosis, called Commerce, has its mental wrecks, too, and no one pays attention; but when a poet falls by the wayside is the chase begun by neurologists and other soul-hunters seeking victims. After the death of Baudelaire's father, the widow, within a year, married the handsome, ambitious Aupick, then chef de bataillon, lieutenant-colonel, decorated with the Legion of Honour, and later general and ambassador to Madrid, Constantinople, and London. Charles was a nervous, frail youth, but unlike most children of genius, he was a scholar and won brilliant honours at school. His stepfather was proud of him. From the Royal College of Lyons, Charles went to the Lycée Louis-le-Grand, Paris, but was expelled in 1839, on various discreditable charges. Troubles soon began at home. He was irascible, vain, precocious, and given to dissipation. He quarreled with General Aupick, and disdained his mother. But she was to blame, she has confessed; she had quite forgotten the boy in the flush of her second love. He could not forget, or forgive what he called her infidelity to the memory of his father. Hamlet-like, he was inconsolable. The good Bishop of Montpellier, who knew the family, said that Charles was a little crazy – second marriages usually bring woe in their train. "When a mother has such a son, she doesn't re-marry," said the young poet Charles signed himself Baudelaire-Dufays, or sometimes Dufais. He wrote in his journal: "My ancestors, idiots or maniacs ... all victims of terrible passions"; which was one of his exaggerations. His grandfather on the paternal side was a Champenois peasant, his mother's family presumably Norman, but not much is known of her forbears. Charles believed himself lost from the time his half-brother was stricken. He also believed that his instability of temperament – and he studied his "case" as would a surgeon – was the result of his parents' disparity in years.

After his return from the East, where he did not learn English as has been said – his mother taught him as a boy to converse in and write the language – he came into his little inheritance, about fifteen thousand dollars. Two years later he was so heavily in debt that his family asked for a guardian on the ground of incompetency. He had been swindled, being young and green. How had he squandered his money? Not exactly on opera-glasses, like Gérard de Nerval, but on clothes, pictures, furniture, books. The remnant was set aside to pay his debts. Charles would be both poet and dandy. He dressed expensively but soberly, in the English fashion; his linen dazzling, the prevailing hue of his habiliments black. In height he was medium, his eyes brown, searching, luminous, the eye of a nyctalops, "eyes like ravens"; nostrils palpitating, cleft chin, mouth expressive, sensual jaw, strong and square. His hair was black, curly, glossy, his forehead high, square and white. In the Deroy portrait he wears a beard;

he is there what Catulle Mendès nicknamed him: "His Excellence, Monseigneur Brummel!" Later he was the elegiac Satan, the author of L'Imitation de N.S. le Diable; or the Baudelaire of George Moore: "the clean-shaven face of the mock priest, the slow cold eyes and the sharp cunning sneer of the cynical libertine who will be tempted that he may better know the worthlessness of temptation." In the heyday of his blood he was perverse and deliberate. Let us credit him with contradicting the Byronic notion that ennui could best be cured by dissipation; in sin Baudelaire found the saddest of all consolations. Mendès laughs at the legend of Baudelaire's violence, of his being given to explosive phrases. Despite Gautier's stories about the Hôtel Pimodan and its club of hasheesh-eaters, M. Mendès denies that Baudelaire was a victim of the hemp. What the majority of mankind does not know concerning the habits of literary workers is this prime fact: men who work hard, writing verse – and there is no mental toil comparable to it – cannot drink, or indulge in opium, without inevitable collapse. The old-fashioned ideas of "inspiration," spontaneity, easy improvisation, the sudden bolt from heaven, are delusions still hugged by the world. To be told that Chopin filed at his music for years, that Beethoven in his smithy forged his thunderbolts by the sweat of his brow, that Manet toiled like a labourer on the dock, that Baudelaire was a mechanic in his devotion to poetic work, that Gautier was a hard-working journalist, are disillusions for the sentimental. Minerva springing full-fledged from Jupiter's skull to the desk of the poet is a pretty fancy; but Balsac and Flaubert did not encourage this fancy. Work literally killed Poe, as it killed Jules de Goncourt, Flaubert and Daudet. Maupassant went insane because he would work and he would play the same day. Baudelaire worked and worried. His debts haunted him his life long. His constitution was flawed – Sainte-Beuve told him that he had worn out his nerves – from the start, he was détraqué; but that his entire life was one huge debauch is a nightmare of the moral police in some red cotton nightcap country.

His period of mental production was not brief nor barren. He was a student. Du Camp's charge that he was an ignorant man is disproved by the variety and quality of his published work. His range of sympathies was large. His mistake, in the eyes of his colleagues, was to write so well about the seven arts. Versatility is seldom given its real name – which is protracted labour. Baudelaire was one of the elect, an aristocrat, who dealt with the quintessence of art; his delicate air of a bishop, his exquisite manners, his modulated voice, aroused unusual interest and admiration. He was a humanist of distinction; he has left a hymn to Saint Francis in the Latin of the decadence. Baudelaire, like Chopin, made more poignant the phrase, raised to a higher intensity the expressiveness of art.

Women played a commanding rôle in his life. They always do with any poet worthy of the name, though few have been so frank in acknowledging this as Baudelaire. Yet he was in love more with Woman than the individual. The legend of the beautiful creature he brought from the East resolves itself into the dismal affair with Jeanne Duval. He met her in Paris, after he had been in the East. She sang at a café concert in Paris. She was more brown than black. She was not handsome, not intelligent, not good; yet he idealized her, for she was the source of half his inspiration. To her were addressed those marvellous evocations of the Orient, of perfume, tresses, delicious dawns on strange far-away seas and "superb Byzant," domes that devils built. Baudelaire is the poet of perfumes; he is also the patron saint of ennui. No one has so chanted the praise of odours. His soul swims on perfume as do other souls on music, he has sung. As he grew older he seemed to hunt for more acrid odours; he often presents an elaborately chased vase the carving of which transports us, but from which the head is quickly averted. Jeanne, whom he never loved, no matter what may be said, was a sorceress. But she was impossible; she robbed, betrayed him; he left her a dozen times only to return. He was a capital draughtsman with a strong nervous line and made many pen-and-ink drawings of her. They are not prepossessing. In her rapid decline she was not allowed to want. Madame Aupick paid her expenses in the hospital. A sordid history. She was a veritable flower of evil for Baudelaire. Yet poetry, like music, would be colourless, scentless, if it sounded no dissonances. Fancy art reduced to the beatific and banal chord of C major!

He fell in love with the celebrated Madame Sabatier, a reigning beauty, at whose salon artistic Paris assembled. She had been christened by Gautier Madame la Présidente, and her sumptuous beauty was portrayed by Ricard in his La Femme au Chien. She returned Baudelaire's love. They soon parted. Again a riddle which the published letters hardly solve. One letter, however, does show that Baudelaire had tried to be faithful, and failed. He could not extort from his exhausted soul the sentiment; but he put its music on paper. His most seductive lyrics were addressed to Madame Sabatier: "A la très chère, à la très-belle," a hymn saturated with love. Music, spleen, perfumes – "colour, sound, perfumes call to each other as deep to deep; perfumes like the flesh of children, soft as hautboys, green as the meadows" – criminals, outcasts, the charm of childhood, the horrors of love, pride, and rebellion, Eastern landscapes, cats, soothing and false; cats, the true companions of lonely poets; haunted clocks, shivering dusks, and gloomier dawns – Paris in a hundred phases – these and many other themes this strange-souled poet, this "Dante, pacer of the shore," of Paris has celebrated in finely wrought verse and profound phrases. In a single line he contrives atmosphere; the very shape of his sentence, the ring of the syllables, arouse the deepest emotion. A master of harmonic undertones is Baudelaire. His successors have excelled him in making their music more fluid, more lyrical, more vapourous – many young French poets pass through their Baudelarian greensickness – but he alone knows the secrets of moulding those metallic, free sonnets, which have the resistance of bronze; and of the despairing music that flames from the mouths of lost souls trembling on the wharves of hell. He is the supreme master of irony and troubled voluptuousness.

Baudelaire is a masculine poet. He carved rather than sang; the plastic arts spoke to his soul. A lover and maker of images. Like Poe, his emotions transformed themselves into ideas. Bourget classified him as mystic, libertine, and analyst. He was born with a wound in his soul, to use the phrase of Père Lacordaire. (Curiously enough, he actually contemplated, in 1861, becoming a candidate for Lacordaire's vacant seat in the French Academy. Sainte-Beuve dissuaded him from this folly.) Recall Baudelaire's prayer: "Thou, O Lord, my God, grant me the grace to produce some fine lines which will prove to myself that I am not the last of men, that I am not inferior to those I contemn." Individualist, egoist, anarchist, his only thought was letters. Jules Laforgue thus described Baudelaire: "Cat, Hindoo, Yankee, Episcopal, Alchemist." Yes, an alchemist who suffocated in the fumes he created. He was of Gothic imagination, and could have said with Rolla: "Je suis venu trop tard dans un monde trop vieux." He had an unassuaged thirst for the absolute. The human soul was his stage, he its interpreting orchestra.

In 1857 The Flowers of Evil was published by Poulet-Malassis, who afterward went into bankruptcy – a warning to publishers with a taste for fine literature. The titles contemplated were Limbes, or Lesbiennes. Hippolyte Babou suggested the one we know. These poems were suppressed on account of six, and poet and publisher summoned. As the municipal government had made a particular ass of itself in the prosecution of Gustave Flaubert and his Madame Bovary, the Baudelaire matter was disposed of in haste. He was condemned to a fine of three hundred francs, a fine which was never paid, as the objectionable poems were removed. They were printed in the Belgian edition, and may be read in the new volume, Œuvres. Posthumes.

Baudelaire was infuriated over the judgment, for he knew that his book was dramatic in expression. He had expected, like Flaubert, to emerge from the trial with flying colours; therefore to be classed as one who wrote objectionable literature was a shock.

"Flaubert had the Empress back of him," he complained; which was true; the Empress Eugénie, also the Princess Mathilde. But he worked as ever and put forth those polished intaglios called Poems in Prose, for the form of which he had taken a hint from Aloys Bertrand's Gaspard de la Nuit. He filled this form with a new content; not alone pictures, but moods, are to be found in those miniatures. Pity is their keynote, a tenderness for the abject and lowly, a revelation of sensibility that surprised those critics who had discerned in Baudelaire only a sculptor of evil. In one of his poems he described a landscape of metal, of marble and water; a babel of staircases and arcades, a palace of infinity, surrounded by the silence of eternity. This depressing yet magical dream was utilized by Huysmans in his A Rebours. But in the tiny landscapes of the Prose Poems there is nothing rigid or artificial. Indeed, the poet's deliberate attitude of artificiality is dropped. He is human. Not that the deep fundamental note of humanity is ever absent in his poems; the eternal diapason is there even when least overheard. Baudelaire is more human than Poe. His range of sympathy is wider. In this he transcends him as a poet, though his subject-matter often issues from the very dregs of life. Brother to pitiable wanderers, there are, nevertheless, no traces of cant, no "Russian pity" à la Dostoiëvsky, no humanitarian or socialistic rhapsodies in his work. Baudelaire is an egoist He hated the sentimental sapping of altruism. His prose-poem, Crowds, with its "bath of multitude," may have been suggested by Poe; but in Charles Lamb we find the idea: "Are there no solitudes out of caves and the desert? or cannot the heart, in the midst of crowds, feel frightfully alone?"

His best critical work is the Richard Wagner and Tannhauser, as significant an essay as Nietzsche's Richard Wagner in Bayreuth. And Baudelaire's polemic appeared at a more critical period in Wagner's career. Wagner sent a brief hearty letter of thanks to the critic, and later made his acquaintance. To Wagner, Baudelaire introduced a young Wagnerian, Villiers de l'Isle Adam. This Wagner letter is included in the volume of Crépet;

but there are no letters published from Baudelaire to Franz Liszt, though they were friends. In Weimar I saw at the Liszt Museum several from Baudelaire which should have been included in the Letters. The poet understood Liszt and his reforms as he understood Wagner. The German composer admired the French poet, and his Kundry, in the sultry second act of Parsifal, has a Baudelairian hue, especially in the temptation scene.

The end was at hand. Baudelaire had been steadily, rather, unsteadily, going downhill; a desperate figure, a dandy in shabby attire. He went out only after dark, he haunted the exterior boulevards, associated with birds of nocturnal plumage. He drank without thirst, ate without hunger, as he has said. A woeful decadence for this aristocrat of life and letters. Most sorrowful of sinners, a morose delectation scourged his nerves and extorted the darkest music from his lyre. He fled to Brussels, there to rehabilitate his dwindling fortunes. He gave a few lectures, and met Rops, Lemonnier, drank to forget, and forgot to work. He abused Brussels, Belgium, its people. A country, he cried, where the trees are black, the flowers without odour, and where there is no conversation! He, the brilliant causeur, the chief blaguer of a circle in which young James McNeill Whistler was reduced to the rôle of a listener – this most spiritual among artists, found himself a failure in the Belgian capital. It may not be amiss to remind ourselves that Baudelaire was the creator of many of the paradoxes attributed, not only to Whistler, but to an entire school – if one may employ such a phrase. The frozen imperturbability of the poet, his cutting enunciation, his power of blasphemy, his hatred of Nature, his love of the artificial, have been copied by the æsthetic blades of our day. He it was who first taunted Nature with being an imitator of art, with always being the same. Oh, the imitative sunsets! Oh, the quotidian eating and drinking! And as pessimist, too, he led the mode. Baudelaire, like Flaubert, grasped the murky torch of pessimism once held by Chateaubriand, Benjamin Constant, and Senancour. Doubtless, all this stemmed from Byronism. And now it is as stale as Byronism.

His health failed, and he lacked money enough to pay for doctor's prescriptions; he even owed for the room in his hotel. At Namur, where he was visiting the father-in-law of Felician Rops (March, 1866), he suffered from an attack of paralysis. He was removed to Brussels. His mother, who lived at Honneur, in mourning for her husband, came to his aid. Taken to France, he was placed in a sanatorium. Aphasia set in. He could only ejaculate a mild oath, and when he caught sight of himself in the mirror he would bow pleasantly as if to a stranger. His friends rallied, and they were among the most distinguished people in Paris, the élite of souls. Ladies visited him, one or two playing Wagner on the piano – which must have added a fresh nuance to death – and they brought him flowers. He expressed his love for flowers and music to the last. He could not bear the sight of his mother; she revived in him some painful memories, but that passed, and he clamoured for her when she was absent. If anyone mentioned the names of Wagner or Manet, he smiled. And with a fixed stare, as if peering through some invisible window opening upon eternity, he died, August 31, 1867, aged forty-six.

Barbey d'Aurevilly himself a Satanist and dandy (oh, those comical old attitudes of literature), had prophesied that the author of Fleurs du Mal would either blow out his brains or prostrate himself at the foot of the cross. (Later he said the same of Huysmans.) Baudelaire had the alternative course forced upon him by fate after he had attempted spiritual suicide for how many years? (He once tried actual suicide, but the slight cut in his throat looked so ugly to him that he went no farther.) His soul had been a battle-field for the powers of good and evil. That at the end he brought the wreck of both soul and body to his God should not be a subject for comment. He was an extraordinary poet with a bad conscience, who lived miserably and was buried with honours. Then it was that his worth was discovered (funeral orations over a genius are a species of public staircase-wit). His reputation waxes with the years. He is an exotic gem in the crown of French poetry. Of him Swinburne has chanted Ave Atque Vale:

Shall I strew on thee rose or rue or laurel,
Brother, on this that was the veil of thee?

Charles Baudelaire by Etienne Carjat, 1863

Charles Baudelaire by Edouard Manet

THE FLOWERS OF EVIL

DANSE MACABRE

A ERNEST CHRISTOPHE

Fière, autant qu'un vivant, de sa noble stature,
Avec son gros bouquet, son mouchoir et ses gants,
Elle a la nonchalance et la désinvolture
D'une coquette maigre aux airs extravagants.

Vit-on jamais au bal une taille plus mince?
Sa robe exagérée, en sa royale ampleur,
S'écroule abondamment sur un pied sec que pince
Un soulier pomponné, joli comme une fleur.

La ruche qui se joue au bord des clavicules,
Comme un ruisseau lascif qui se frotte au rocher,
Défend pudiquement des lazzi ridicules
Les funèbres appas qu'elle tient à cacher.

Ses yeux profonds sont faits de vide et de ténèbres
Et son crâne, de fleurs artistement coiffé,
Oscille mollement sur ses frêles vertèbres.
—O charme d'un néant follement attifé!

Aucuns t'appelleront une caricature,
Qui ne comprennent pas, amants ivres de chair,
L'élégance sans nom de l'humaine armature.
Tu réponds, grand squelette, à mon goût le plus cher!

Viens-tu troubler, avec ta puissante grimace,
La fête de la Vie? ou quelque vieux désir,
Eperonnant encor ta vivante carcasse,
Te pousse-t-il, crédule, au sabbat du Plaisir?

Au chant des violons, aux flammes des bougies,
Espères-tu chasser ton cauchemar moqueur,
Et viens-tu demander au torrent des orgies
De refraîchir l'enfer allumé dans ton cœur?

Inépuisable puits de sottise et de fautes!
De l'antique douleur éternel alambic!
A travers le treillis recourbé de tes côtes
Je vois, errant encor, l'insatiable aspic.

Pour dire vrai, je crains que ta coquetterie
Ne trouve pas un prix digne de ses efforts:
Qui, de ces cœurs mortels, entend la raillerie?
Les charmes de l'horreur n'enivrent que les forts.

Le gouffre de tes yeux, plein d'horribles pensées,
Exalte le vertige, et les danseurs prudents
Ne contempleront pas sans d'amères nausées
Le sourire éternel de tes trente-deux dents.

Pourtant, qui n'a serré dans ses bras un squelette,
Et qui ne s'est nourri des choses du tombeau?
Qu'importé le parfum, l'habit ou la toilette?
Qui fait le dégoûté montre qu'il se croit beau.

Bayadère sans nez, irrésistible gouge,
Dis donc à ces danseurs qui font les offusqués:
« Fiers mignons, malgré l'art des poudres et du rouge,
Vous sentez tous la mort! O squelettes musqués,

Antinoüs flétris, dandys à face glabre,
Cadavres vernissés, lovelaces chenus,
Le branle universel de la danse macabre
Vous entraîne en des lieux qui ne sont pas connus!

Des quais froids de la Seine aux bords brûlants du Gange,
Le troupeau mortel saute et se pâme, sans voir
Dans un trou du plafond la trompette de l'Ange
Sinistrement béante ainsi qu'un tromblon noir.

En tout climat, sous ton soleil, la Mort t'admire
En tes contorsions, risible Humanité,
Et souvent, comme toi, se parfumant de myrrhe,
Mêle son ironie à ton insanité! »

THE DANCE OF DEATH

Carrying bouquet, and handkerchief, and gloves,
Proud of her height as when she lived, she moves
With all the careless and high-stepping grace,
And the extravagant courtesan's thin face.

Was slimmer waist e'er in a ball-room wooed?
Her floating robe, in royal amplitude,
Palls in deep folds around a dry foot, shod
With a bright flower-like shoe that gems the sod.

The swarms that hum about her collar-bones
As the lascivious streams caress the stones,
Conceal from every scornful jest that flies,
Her gloomy beauty; and her fathomless eyes

Are made of shade and void; with flowery sprays
Her skull is wreathed artistically, and sways,
Feeble and weak, on her frail vertebræ.
O charm of nothing decked in folly! they

Who laugh and name you a Caricature,
They see not, they whom flesh and blood allure,
The nameless grace of every bleached, bare bone
That is most dear to me, tall skeleton!

Come you to trouble with your potent sneer
The feast of Life! or are you driven here,
To Pleasure's Sabbath, by dead lusts that stir
And goad your moving corpse on with a spur?

Or do you hope, when sing the violins,
And the pale candle-flame lights up our sins,

To drive some mocking nightmare far apart,
And cool the flame hell lighted in your heart?

Fathomless well of fault and foolishness!
Eternal alembic of antique distress!
Still o'er the curved, white trellis of your sides
The sateless, wandering serpent curls and glides.

And truth to tell, I fear lest you should find,
Among us here, no lover to your mind;
Which of these hearts beat for the smile you gave?
The charms of horror please none but the brave.

Your eyes' black gulf, where awful broodings stir,
Brings giddiness; the prudent reveller
Sees, while a horror grips him from beneath,
The eternal smile of thirty-two white teeth.

For he who has not folded in his arms
A skeleton, nor fed on graveyard charms,
Recks not of furbelow, or paint, or scent,
When Horror comes the way that Beauty went.

O irresistible, with fleshless face,
Say to these dancers in their dazzled race:
"Proud lovers with the paint above your bones,
Ye shall taste death, musk-scented skeletons!

Withered Antinous, dandies with plump faces,
Ye varnished cadavers, and grey Lovelaces,
Ye go to lands unknown and void of breath,
Drawn by the rumour of the Dance of Death.

From Seine's cold quays to Ganges' burning stream,
The mortal troupes dance onward in a dream;

They do not see, within the opened sky,
The Angel's sinister trumpet raised on high.

In every clime and under every sun,
Death laughs at ye, mad mortals, as ye run;
And oft perfumes herself with myrrh, like ye
And mingles with your madness, irony!"

LES PHARES

Rubens, fleuve d'oubli, jardin de la paresse,
Oreiller de chair fraîche où l'on ne peut aimer,
Mais où la vie afflue et s'agite sans cesse,
Comme l'air dans le ciel et la mer dans la mer;

Léonard de Vinci, miroir profond et sombre,
Où des anges charmants, avec un doux souris
Tout chargé de mystère, apparaissent à l'ombre
Des glaciers et des pins qui ferment leur pays;

Rembrandt, triste hôpital tout rempli de murmures,
Et d'un grand crucifix décoré seulement,
Où la prière en pleurs s'exhale des ordures,
Et d'un rayon d'hiver traversé brusquement;

Michel-Ange, lieu vague où l'on voit des Hercules
Se mêler à des Christ, et se lever tout droits
Des fantômes puissants, qui dans les crépuscules
Déchirent leur suaire en étirant leurs doigts;

Colères de boxeur, impudences de faune,
Toi qui sus ramasser la beauté des goujats,
Grand cœur gonflé d'orgueil, homme débile et jaune,
Puget, mélancolique empereur des forçats;

Watteau, ce carnaval où bien des cœurs illustres,
Comme des papillons, errent en flamboyant,
Décors frais et légers éclairés par des lustres
Qui versent la folie à ce bal tournoyant;

Goya, cauchemar plein de choses inconnues,
De fœtus qu'on fait cuire au milieu des sabbats,

De vieilles au miroir et d'enfants toutes nues,
Pour tenter les Démons ajustant bien leurs bas;

Delacroix, lac de sang hanté des mauvais anges,
Ombragé par un bois de sapin toujours vert,
Où, sous un ciel chagrin, des fanfares étranges
Passent, comme un soupir étouffé de Weber;

Ces malédictions, ces blasphèmes, ces plaintes,
Ces extases, ces cris, ces pleurs, ces *Te Deum,*
Sont un écho redit par mille labyrinthes;
C'est pour les cœurs mortels un divin opium.

C'est un cri répété par mille sentinelles,
Un ordre renvoyé par mille porte-voix;
C'est un phare allumé sur mille citadelles,
Un appel de chasseurs perdus dans les grands bois!

Car c'est vraiment, Seigneur, le meilleur témoignage
Que nous puissions donner de notre dignité
Que cet ardent sanglot qui roule d'âge en âge
Et vient mourir au bord de votre éternité!

THE BEACONS

RUBENS, oblivious garden of indolence,
    Pillow of cool flesh where no man dreams of love,
Where life flows forth in troubled opulence,
    As airs in heaven and seas in ocean move,

LEONARD DA VINCI, sombre and fathomless glass,
    Where lovely angels with calm lips that smile,
Heavy with mystery, in the shadow pass,
    Among the ice and pines that guard some isle.

REMBRANDT, sad hospital that a murmuring fills,
    Where one tall crucifix hangs on the walls,
Where every tear-drowned prayer some woe distils,
    And one cold, wintry ray obliquely falls.

Strong MICHELANGELO, a vague far place
    Where mingle Christs with pagan Hercules;
Thin phantoms of the great through twilight pace,
    And tear their shroud with clenched hands void of ease.

The fighter's anger, the faun's impudence,
    Thou makest of all these a lovely thing;
Proud heart, sick body, mind's magnificence:
    PUGET, the convict's melancholy king.

WATTEAU, the carnival of illustrious hearts,
    Fluttering like moths upon the wings of chance;
Bright lustres light the silk that flames and darts,
    And pour down folly on the whirling dance.

GOYA, a nightmare full of things unknown;
    The fœtus witches broil on Sabbath night;

Old women at the mirror; children lone
    Who tempt old demons with their limbs delight.

DELACROIX, lake of blood ill angels haunt,
    Where ever-green, o'ershadowing woods arise;
Under the surly heaven strange fanfares chaunt
    And pass, like one of Weber's strangled sighs.

And malediction, blasphemy and groan,
    Ecstasies, cries, Te Deums, and tears of brine,
Are echoes through a thousand labyrinths flown;
    For mortal hearts an opiate divine;

A shout cried by a thousand sentinels,
    An order from a thousand bugles tossed,
A beacon o'er a thousand citadels,
    A call to huntsmen in deep woodlands lost.

It is the mightiest witness that could rise
    To prove our dignity, O Lord, to Thee;
This sob that rolls from age to age, and dies
    Upon the verge of Thy Eternity!

TRISTESSE DE LA LUNE

Ce soir, la lune rêve avec plus de paresse;
Ainsi qu'une beauté, sur de nombreux coussins,
Qui d'une main distraite et légère caresse,
Avant de s'endormir, le contour de ses seins,

Sur le dos satiné des molles avalanches,
Mourante, elle se livre aux longues pâmoisons,
Et promène ses yeux sur les visions blanches
Qui montent dans l'azur comme des floraisons.

Quand parfois sur ce globe, en sa langueur oisive,
Elle laisse filer une larme furtive,
Un poète pieux, ennemi du sommeil,

Dans le creux de sa main prend cette larme pâle,
Aux reflets irisés comme un fragment d'opale,
Et la met dans son cœur loin des yeux du soleil.

THE SADNESS OF THE MOON

The Moon more indolently dreams to-night
Than a fair woman on her couch at rest.
Caressing, with a hand distraught and light,
Before she sleeps, the contour of her breast.

Upon her silken avalanche of down,
Dying she breathes a long and swooning sigh;
And watches the white visions past her flown,
Which rise like blossoms to the azure sky.

And when, at times, wrapped in her languor deep,
Earthward she lets a furtive tear-drop flow,
Some pious poet, enemy of sleep,

Takes in his hollow hand the tear of snow
Whence gleams of iris and of opal start,
And hides it from the Sun, deep in his heart.

PARFUM EXOTIQUE

Quand, les deux yeux fermés, en un soir chaud d'automne,
Je respire l'odeur de ton sein chaleureux,
Je vois se dérouler des rivages heureux
Qu'éblouissent les feux d'un soleil monotone;

Une île paresseuse où la nature donne
Des arbres singuliers et des fruits savoureux;
Des hommes dont le corps est mince et vigoureux,
Et des femmes dont l'œil, par sa franchise, étonne.

Guidé par ton odeur vers de charmants climats,
Je vois un port rempli de voiles et de mâts
Encor tout fatigués par la vague marine,

Pendant que le parfum des verts tamariniers,
Qui circule dans l'air et m'enfle la narine.
Se mêle dans mon âme au chant des mariniers.

EXOTIC PERFUME

When with closed eyes in autumn's eves of gold
    I breathe the burning odours of your breast,
    Before my eyes the hills of happy rest
Bathed in the sun's monotonous fires, unfold.

Islands of Lethe where exotic boughs
    Bend with their burden of strange fruit bowed down.
    Where men are upright, maids have never grown
Unkind, but bear a light upon their brows.

Led by that perfume to these lands of ease,
I see a port where many ships have flown
With sails outwearied of the wandering seas;

While the faint odours from green tamarisks blown,
Float to my soul and in my senses throng,
And mingle vaguely with the sailor's song.

LA BEAUTÉ

Je suis belle, ô mortels! comme un rêve de pierre,
Et mon sein, où chacun s'est meurtri tour à tour,
Est fait pour inspirer au poète un amour
Eternel et muet ainsi que la matière.

Je trône dans l'azur comme un sphinx incompris;
J'unis un cœur de neige à la blancheur des cygnes;
Je hais le mouvement qui déplace les lignes,
Et jamais je ne pleure et jamais je ne ris.

Les poètes, devant mes grandes attitudes.
Que j'ai l'air d'emprunter aux plus fiers monuments,
Consumeront leurs jours en d'austères études;

Car j'ai, pour fasciner ces dociles amants,
De purs miroirs qui font toutes choses plus belles:
Mes yeux, mes larges yeux aux clartés éternelles!

BEAUTY

I am as lovely as a dream in stone,
And this my heart where each finds death in turn,
Inspires the poet with a love as lone
As clay eternal and as taciturn.

Swan-white of heart, a sphinx no mortal knows,
My throne is in the heaven's azure deep;
I hate all movements that disturb my pose,
I smile not ever, neither do I weep.

Before my monumental attitudes,
That breathe a soul into the plastic arts,
My poets pray in austere studious moods,

For I, to fold enchantment round their hearts,
Have pools of light where beauty flames and dies,
The placid mirrors of my luminous eyes.

LE BALCON

Mère des souvenirs, maîtresse des maîtresses,
O toi, tous mes plaisirs, ô toi, tous mes devoirs!
Tu te rappelleras la beauté des caresses,
La douceur du foyer et le charme des soirs,
Mère des souvenirs, maîtresse des maîtresses!

Les soirs illuminés par l'ardeur du charbon,
Et les soirs au balcon, voilés de vapeurs roses;
Que ton sein m'était doux! que ton cœur m'était bon!
Nous avons dit souvent d'impérissables choses
Les soirs illuminés par l'ardeur du charbon.

Que les soleils sont beaux dans les chaudes soirées!
Que l'espace est profond! que le cœur est puissant!
En me penchant vers toi, reine des adorées,
Je croyais respirer le parfum de ton sang.
Que les soleils sont beaux dans les chaudes soirées!

La nuit s'épaississait ainsi qu'une cloison,
Et mes yeux dans le noir devinaient tes prunelles
Et je buvais ton souffle, ô douceur, ô poison!
Et tes pieds s'endormaient dans mes mains fraternelles,
La nuit s'épaississait ainsi qu'une cloison.

Je sais l'art d'évoquer les minutes heureuses,
Et revis mon passé blotti dans tes genoux.
Car à quoi bon chercher tes beautés langoureuses
Ailleurs qu'en ton cher corps et qu'en ton cœur si doux?
Je sais l'art d'évoquer les minutes heureuses!

Ces serments, ces parfums, ces baisers infinis,
Renaîtront-ils d'un gouffre interdit à nos sondes,

Comme montent au ciel les soleils rajeunis
Après s'être lacés au fond des mers profondes!
– O serments! ô parfums! ô baisers infinis!

THE BALCONY

Mother of memories, mistress of mistresses,
    O thou, my pleasure, thou, all my desire,
Thou shalt recall the beauty of caresses,
    The charm of evenings by the gentle fire,
Mother of memories, mistress of mistresses!

The eves illumined by the burning coal,
    The balcony where veiled rose-vapour clings –
How soft your breast was then, how sweet your soul!
    Ah, and we said imperishable things,
Those eves illumined by the burning coal.

Lovely the suns were in those twilights warm,
    And space profound, and strong life's pulsing flood,
In bending o'er you, queen of every charm,
    I thought I breathed the perfume in your blood.
The suns were beauteous in those twilights warm.

The film of night flowed round and over us,
    And my eyes in the dark did your eyes meet;
I drank your breath, ah! sweet and poisonous,
    And in my hands fraternal slept your feet –
Night, like a film, flowed round and over us.

I can recall those happy days forgot,
    And see, with head bowed on your knees, my past.
Your languid beauties now would move me not
    Did not your gentle heart and body cast
The old spell of those happy days forgot.

Can vows and perfumes, kisses infinite,
    Be reborn from the gulf we cannot sound;

As rise to heaven suns once again made bright
    After being plunged in deep seas and profound?
Ah, vows and perfumes, kisses infinite!

LA MUSE MALADE

Ma pauvre Muse, hélas! qu'as-tu donc ce matin?
Tes yeux creux sont peuplés de visions nocturnes,
Et je vois tour à tour s'étaler sur ton teint
La folie et l'horreur, froides et taciturnes.

Le succube verdâtre et le rose lutin
T'ont-ils versé la peur et l'amour de leurs urnes?
Le cauchemar, d'un poing despotique et mutin,
T'a-t-il noyée au fond d'un fabuleux Minturnes?

Je voudrais qu'exhalant l'odeur de la santé
Ton sein de pensers forts fût toujours fréquenté,
Et que ton sang chrétien coulât à flots rythmiques

Comme les sons nombreux des syllabes antiques,
Où règnent tour à tour le père des chansons,
Phœbus, et le grand Pan, le seigneur des moissons.

THE SICK MUSE

Poor Muse, alas, what ails thee, then, to-day?
Thy hollow eyes with midnight visions burn,
Upon thy brow in alternation play,
Folly and Horror, cold and taciturn.

Have the green lemure and the goblin red,
Poured on thee love and terror from their urn?
Or with despotic hand the nightmare dread
Deep plunged thee in some fabulous Minturne?

Would that thy breast where so deep thoughts arise,
Breathed forth a healthful perfume with thy sighs;
Would that thy Christian blood ran wave by wave

In rhythmic sounds the antique numbers gave,
When Phœbus shared his alternating reign
With mighty Pan, lord of the ripening grain.

LA MUSE VENALE

O Muse de mon cœur, amante des palais,
Auras-tu, quand Janvier lâchera ses Borées,
Durant les noirs ennuis des neigeuses soirées,
Un tison pour chauffer tes deux pieds violets?

Ranimeras-tu donc tes épaules marbrées
Aux nocturnes rayons qui percent les volets?
Sentant ta bourse à sec autant que ton palais,
Récolteras-tu l'or des voûtes azurées?

Il te faut, pour gagner ton pain de chaque soir,
Comme un enfant de choeur, jouer de l'encensoir,
Chantes des *Te Deum* auxquels tu ne crois guère,

Ou, saltimbanque à jeun, étaler les appas
Et ton rire trempé de pleurs qu'on ne voit pas,
Pour faire épanouir la rate du vulgaire.

THE VENAL MUSE

Muse of my heart, lover of palaces,
    When January comes with wind and sleet,
During the snowy eve's long wearinesses,
    Will there be fire to warm thy violet feet?

Wilt thou reanimate thy marble shoulders
    In the moon-beams that through the window fly?
Or when thy purse dries up, thy palace moulders,
    Reap the far star-gold of the vaulted sky?

For thou, to keep thy body to thy soul,
Must swing a censer, wear a holy stole,
    And chaunt Te Deums with unbelief between.

Or, like a starving mountebank, expose
Thy beauty and thy tear-drowned smile to those
    Who wait thy jeste to drive away thy spleen.

LE MAUVAIS MOINE

Les cloîtres anciens sur les grandes murailles
Étalaient en tableaux la sainte Vérité,
Dont l'effet, réchauffant les pieuses entrailles,
Tempérait la froideur de leur austérité.

En ces temps où du Christ florissaient les semailles
Plus d'un illustre moine, aujourd'hui peu cité,
Prenant pour atelier le champ des funérailles,
Glorifiait la Mort avec simplicité.

Mon âme est un tombeau que, mauvais cénobite,
Depuis l'éternité je parcours et j'habite;
Rien n'embellit les murs de ce cloître odieux.

O moine fainéant! quand saurai-je donc faire
Du spectacle vivant de ma triste misère
Le travail de mes mains et l'amour de mes yeux?

THE EVIL MONK

The ancient cloisters on their lofty walls
    Had holy Truth in painted frescoes shown,
And, seeing these, the pious in those halls
    Felt their cold, lone austereness less alone.

At that time when Christ's seed flowered all around,
    More than one monk, forgotten in his hour,
Taking for studio the burial-ground,
    Glorified Death with simple faith and power.

And my soul is a sepulchre where I,
Ill cenobite, have spent eternity:
    On the vile cloister walls no pictures rise.

O when may I cast off this weariness,
And make the pageant of my old distress
    For these hands labour, pleasure for these eyes?

TOUT ENTIERE

Le Démon, dans ma chambre haute,
Ce matin est venu me voir,
Et, tâchant à me prendre en faute,
Me dit: « Je voudrais bien savoir,

Parmi toutes les belles choses
Dont est fait son enchantement,
Parmi les objets noirs ou roses
Qui composent son corps charmant,

Quel est le plus doux. » – O mon âme!
Tu répondis à l'Abhorré:
« Puisqu'en elle tout est dictame,
Rien ne peut être préféré.

Lorsque tout me ravit, j'ignore
Si quelque chose me séduit.
Elle éblouit comme l'Aurore
Et console comme la Nuit;

Et l'harmonie est trop exquise,
Qui gouverne tout son beau corps,
Pour que l'impuissante analyse
En note les nombreux accords.

O métamorphose mystique
De tous mes sens fondus en un!
Son haleine fait la musique,
Comme sa voix fait le parfum! »

THE TEMPTATION

The Demon, in my chamber high.
    This morning came to visit me,
And, thinking he would find some fault,
    He whispered: "I would know of thee

Among the many lovely things
    That make the magic of her face,
Among the beauties, black and rose,
    That make her body's charm and grace,

Which is most fair?" Thou didst reply
    To the Abhorred, O soul of mine:
"No single beauty is the best
    When she is all one flower divine.

When all things charm me I ignore
    Which one alone brings most delight;
She shines before me like the dawn,
    And she consoles me like the night.

The harmony is far too great,
    That governs all her body fair,
For impotence to analyse
    And say which note is sweetest there.

O mystic metamorphosis!
    My senses into one sense flow –
Her voice makes perfume when she speaks,
    Her breath is music faint and low!"

L'IRREPARABLE

I

Pouvons-nous étouffer le vieux, le long Remords,
    Qui vit, s'agite et se tortille,
Et se nourrit de nous comme le ver des morts,
    Comme du chêne la chenille?
Pouvons-nous étouffer l'implacable Remords?

Dans quel philtre, dans quel vin, dans quelle tisane
    Noierons-nous ce vieil ennemi,
Destructeur et gourmand comme la courtisane,
    Patient comme la fourmi?
Dans quel philtre? — dans quel vin? — dans quelle tisane?

Dis-le, belle sorcière, oh! dis, si tu le sais,
    A cet esprit comblé d'angoisse
Et pareil au mourant qu'écrasent les blessés,
    Que le sabot du cheval froisse,
Dis-le, belle sorcière, oh! dis, si tu le sais,

A cet agonisant que le loup déjà flaire
    Et que surveille le corbeau,
A ce soldat brisé, s'il faut qu'il désespère
    D'avoir sa croix et son tombeau;
Ce pauvre agonisant que le loup déjà flaire!

Peut-on illuminer un ciel bourbeux et noir?
    Peut-on déchirer des ténèbres
Plus denses que la poix, sans matin et sans soir,
    Sans astres, sans éclairs funèbres?
Peut-on illuminer un ciel bourbeux et noir?

L'Espérance qui brille aux carreaux de l'Auberge
    Est souillée, est morte à jamais!
Sans lune et sans rayons trouver où l'on héberge
    Les martyrs d'un chemin mauvais!
Le Diable a tout éteint aux carreaux de l'Auberge!

Adorable sorcière, aimes-tu les damnés!
    Dis, connais-tu l'irrémissible?
Connais-tu le Remords, aux traits empoisonnés,
    A qui notre cœur sert de cible?
Adorable sorcière, aimes-tu les damnés?

L'irréparable ronge avec sa dent maudite
    Notre âme, piteux monument,
Et souvent il attaque, ainsi que le termite,
    Par la base le bâtiment.
L'irréparable ronge avec sa dent maudite!

THE IRREPARABLE

I

Can we suppress the old Remorse
    Who bends our heart beneath his stroke,
Who feeds, as worms feed on the corse,
    Or as the acorn on the oak?
Can we suppress the old Remorse!

Ah, in what philtre, wine, or spell,
    May we drown this our ancient foe,
Destructive glutton, gorging well,
    Patient as the ants, and slow?
What wine, what philtre, or what spell?

Tell it, enchantress, if you can,
    Tell me, with anguish overcast,
Wounded, as a dying man,
    Beneath the swift hoofs hurrying past.
Tell it, enchantress, if you can,

To him the wolf already tears
    Who sees the carrion pinions wave,
This broken warrior who despairs
    To have a cross above his grave –
This wretch the wolf already tears.

Can one illume a leaden sky,
    Or tear apart the shadowy veil
Thicker than pitch, no star on high,
    Not one funereal glimmer pale
Can one illume a leaden sky?

Hope lit the windows of the Inn,
    But now that shining flame is dead;
And how shall martyred pilgrims win
    Along the moonless road they tread?
Satan has darkened all the Inn!

Witch, do you love accursèd hearts?
    Say, do you know the reprobate?
Know you Remorse, whose venomed darts
    Make souls the targets for their hate?
Witch, do you know accursèd hearts?

The Might-have-been with tooth accursed
    Gnaws at the piteous souls of men,
The deep foundations suffer first,
    And all the structure crumbles then
Beneath the bitter tooth accursed.

II

Often, when seated at the play,
    And sonorous music lights the stage,
I see the frail hand of a Fay
    With magic dawn illume the rage
Of the dark sky. Oft at the play

A being made of gauze and fire
    Casts to the earth a Demon great.
And my heart, whence all hopes expire,
    Is like a stage where I await,
In vain, the Fay with wings of fire!

LA VIE ANTERIEURE

J'ai longtemps habité sous de vastes portiques
Que les soleils marins teignaient de mille feux,
Et que leurs grands piliers, droits et majestueux,
Rendaient pareils, le soir, aux grottes basaltiques.

Les houles, en roulant les images des cieux,
Mêlaient d'une façon solennelle et mystique
Les tout-puissants accords de leur riche musique
Aux couleurs du couchant reflété par mes yeux.

C'est là que j'ai vécu dans les voluptés calmes,
Au milieu de l'azur, des vagues, des splendeurs
Et des esclaves nus, tout imprégnés d'odeurs,

Qui me rafraîchissaient le front avec des palmes,
Et dont l'unique soin était d'approfondir
Le secret douloureux qui me faisait languir.

A FORMER LIFE

Long since, I lived beneath vast porticoes,
By many ocean-sunsets tinged and fired,
Where mighty pillars, in majestic rows,
Seemed like basaltic caves when day expired.

The rolling surge that mirrored all the skies
Mingled its music, turbulent and rich,
Solemn and mystic, with the colours which
The setting sun reflected in my eyes.

And there I lived amid voluptuous calms,
In splendours of blue sky and wandering wave,
Tended by many a naked, perfumed slave,

Who fanned my languid brow with waving palms.
They were my slaves – the only care they had
To know what secret grief had made me sad.

DON JUAN AUX ENFERS

Quand don Juan descendit vers l'onde souterraine,
Et lorsqu'il eut donné son obole à Charon,
Un sombre mendiant, l'œil fier comme Antisthène,
D'un bras vengeur et fort saisit chaque aviron.

Montrant leurs seins pendants et leurs robes ouvertes,
Des femmes se tordaient sous le noir firmament,
Et, comme un grand troupeau de victimes offertes,
Derrière lui traînaient un long mugissement.

Sganarelle en riant lui réclamait ses gages,
Tandis que don Luis avec un doigt tremblant
Montrait à tous les morts errant sur les rivages
Le fils audacieux qui railla son front blanc.

Frissonnant sous son deuil, la chaste et maigre Elvire,
Près de l'époux perfide et qui fui son amant
Semblait lui réclamer un suprême sourire
Où brillât la douceur de son premier serment.

Tout droit dans son armure, un grand homme de pierre
Se tenait à la barre et coupait le flot noir;
Mais le calme héros, courbé sur sa rapière,
Regardait le sillage et ne daignait rien voir.

DON JUAN IN HADES

When Juan sought the subterranean flood.
    And paid his obolus on the Stygian shore.
Charon, the proud and sombre beggar, stood
    With one strong, vengeful hand on either oar.

With open robes and bodies agonised,
    Lost women writhed beneath that darkling sky;
There were sounds as of victims sacrificed:
    Behind him all the dark was one long cry.

And Sganarelle, with laughter, claimed his pledge;
    Don Luis, with trembling finger in the air,
Showed to the souls who wandered in the sedge
    The evil son who scorned his hoary hair.

Shivering with woe, chaste Elvira the while,
    Near him untrue to all but her till now,
Seemed to beseech him for one farewell smile
    Lit with the sweetness of the first soft vow.

And clad in armour, a tall man of stone
    Held firm the helm, and clove the gloomy flood;
But, staring at the vessel's track alone,
    Bent on his sword the unmoved hero stood.

LE FLAMBEAU VIVANT

Ils marchent devant moi, ces Yeux pleins de lumières,
Qu'un Ange très savant a sans doute aimantés;
Ils marchent, ces divins frères qui sont mes frères,
Secouant dans mes yeux leurs feux diamantés.

Me sauvant de tout piège et de tout péché grave,
Ils conduisent mes pas dans la route du beau;
Ils sont mes serviteurs, et je suis leur esclave;
Tout mon être obéit à ce vivant flambeau.

Charmants Yeux, vous brillez de la clarté mystique
Qu'ont les cierges brûlant en plein jour; le soleil
Rougit, mais n'éteint pas leur flamme fantastique;

Ils célèbrent la Mort, vous chantez le Réveil;
Vous marchez en chantant le réveil de mon âme,
Astres dont nul soleil ne peut flétrir la flamme!

THE LIVING FLAME

They pass before me, these Eyes full of light,
Eyes made magnetic by some angel wise;
The holy brothers pass before my sight,
And cast their diamond fires in my dim eyes.

They keep me from all sin and error grave,
They set me in the path whence Beauty came;
They are my servants, and I am their slave,
And all my soul obeys the living flame.

Beautiful Eyes that gleam with mystic light
As candles lighted at full noon; the sun
Dims not your flame phantastical and bright.

You sing the dawn; they celebrate life done;
Marching you chaunt my soul's awakening hymn,
Stars that no sun has ever made grow dim!

CORRESPONDANCES

La Nature est un temple où de vivants piliers
Laissent parfois sortir de confuses paroles;
L'homme y passe à travers des forêts de symboles
Qui l'observent avec des regards familiers.

Comme de longs échos qui de loin se confondent
Dans une ténébreuse et profonde unité,
Vaste comme la nuit et comme la clarté,
Les parfums, les couleurs et les sons se répondent.

Il est des parfums frais comme des chairs d'enfants,
Doux comme les hautbois, verts comme les prairies;
Et d'autres, corrompus, riches et triomphants,

Ayant l'expansion des choses infinies,
Comme l'ambre, le musc, le benjoin et l'encens,
Qui chantent les transports de l'esprit et des sens.

CORRESPONDENCES

In Nature's temple living pillars rise,
    And words are murmured none have understood.
    And man must wander through a tangled wood
Of symbols watching him with friendly eyes.

As long-drawn echoes heard far-off and dim
    Mingle to one deep sound and fade away;
    Vast as the night and brilliant as the day,
Colour and sound and perfume speak to him.

Some perfumes are as fragrant as a child,
    Sweet as the sound of hautboys, meadow-green;
Others, corrupted, rich, exultant, wild,

Have all the expansion of things infinite:
    As amber, incense, musk, and benzoin,
Which sing the sense's and the soul's delight.

LE FLACON

Il est de forts parfums pour qui toute matière
Est poreuse. On dirait qu'ils pénètrent le verre.
En ouvrant un coffret venu de l'orient
Dont la serrure grince et rechigne en criant,

Ou dans une maison déserte quelque armoire
Pleine de l'âcre odeur des temps, poudreuse et noire,
Parfois on trouve un vieux flacon qui se souvient,
D'où jaillit toute vive une âme qui revient.

Mille pensers dormaient, chrysalides funèbres,
Frémissant doucement dans tes lourdes ténèbres,
Qui dégagent leur aile et prennent leur essor,
Teintés d'azur, glacés de rose, lamés d'or.

Voilà le souvenir enivrant qui voltige
Dans l'air troublé; les yeux se ferment; le Vertige
Saisit l'âme vaincue et la pousse à deux mains
Vers un gouffre obscurci de miasmes humains;

Il la terrasse au bord d'un gouffre séculaire,
Où, Lazare odorant déchirant son suaire,
Se meut dans son réveil le cadavre spectral
D'un vieil amour ranci, charmant et sépulcral.

Ainsi, quand je serai perdu dans la mémoire
Des hommes, dans le coin d'une sinistre armoire;
Quand on m'aura jeté, vieux flacon désolé,
Décrépit, poudreux, sale, abject, visqueux, fêlé,

Je serai ton cercueil, aimable pestilence!
Le témoin de ta force et de ta virulence,

Cher poison préparé par les anges! liqueur
Qui me ronge, ô la vie et la mort de mon cœur!

THE FLASK

There are some powerful odours that can pass
Out of the stoppered flagon; even glass
To them is porous. Oft when some old box
Brought from the East is opened and the locks
And hinges creak and cry; or in a press
In some deserted house, where the sharp stress
Of odours old and dusty fills the brain;
An ancient flask is brought to light again,
And forth the ghosts of long-dead odours creep.
There, softly trembling in the shadows, sleep
A thousand thoughts, funereal chrysalides,
Phantoms of old the folding darkness hides,
Who make faint flutterings as their wings unfold,
Rose-washed and azure-tinted, shot with gold.
A memory that brings languor flutters here:
The fainting eyelids droop, and giddy Fear
Thrusts with both hands the soul towards the pit
Where, like a Lazarus from his winding-sheet,
Arises from the gulf of sleep a ghost
Of an old passion, long since loved and lost.
So I, when vanished from man's memory
Deep in some dark and sombre chest I lie.
An empty flagon they have cast aside,
Broken and soiled, the dust upon my pride,
Will be your shroud, beloved pestilence!
The witness of your might and virulence,
Sweet poison mixed by angels; bitter cup
Of life and death my heart has drunken up!

RÉVERSIBILITÉ

Ange plein de gaieté, connaissez-vous l'angoisse,
    La honte, les remords, les sanglots, les ennuis,
    Et les vagues terreurs de ces affreuses nuits
Qui compriment le cœur comme un papier qu'on froisse?
Ange plein de gaieté, connaissez-vous l'angoisse?

Ange plein de bonté, connaissez-vous la haine,
    Les poings crispés dans l'ombre et les larmes de fiel,
    Quand la Vengeance bat son infernal rappel,
Et de nos facultés se fait le capitaine?
Ange plein de bonté connaissez-vous la haine?

Ange plein de santé, connaissez-vous les Fièvres,
    Qui, le long des grands murs de l'hospice blafard,
    Comme des exilés, s'en vont d'un pied traînard,
Cherchant le soleil rare et remuant les lèvres?
Ange plein de santé, connaissez-vous les Fièvres?

Ange plein de beauté, connaissez-vous les rides,
    Et la peur de vieillir, et ce hideux tourment
    De lire la secrète horreur du dévouement
Dans des yeux où longtemps burent nos yeux avides!
Ange plein de beauté, connaissez-vous les rides?

Ange plein de bonheur, de joie et de lumières,
    David mourant aurait demandé la santé
    Aux émanations de ton corps enchanté;
Mais de toi je n'implore, ange, que tes prières,
Ange plein de bonheur, de joie et de lumières!

REVERSIBILITY

Angel of gaiety, have you tasted grief?
    Shame and remorse and sobs and weary spite,
    And the vague terrors of the fearful night
That crush the heart up like a crumpled leaf?
Angel of gaiety, have you tasted grief?

Angel of kindness, have you tasted hate?
    With hands clenched in the shade and tears of gall,
    When Vengeance beats her hellish battle-call,
And makes herself the captain of our fate,
Angel of kindness, have you tasted hate?

Angel of health, did ever you know pain,
    Which like an exile trails his tired footfalls
    The cold length of the white infirmary walls,
With lips compressed, seeking the sun in vain?
Angel of health, did ever you know pain?

Angel of beauty, do you wrinkles know?
    Know you the fear of age, the torment vile
    Of reading secret horror in the smile
Of eyes your eyes have loved since long ago?
Angel of beauty, do you wrinkles know?

Angel of happiness, and joy, and light,
    Old David would have asked for youth afresh
    From the pure touch of your enchanted flesh;
I but implore your prayers to aid my plight,
Angel of happiness, and joy, and light.

CAUSERIE

Vous êtes un beau ciel d'automne, clair et rose!
Mais la tristesse en moi monte comme la mer,
Et laisse, en refluant, sur ma lèvre morose
Le souvenir cuisant de son limon amer.

 – Ta main se glisse en vain sur mon sein qui se pâme;
Ce qu'elle cherche, amie, est un lieu saccagé
Par la griffe et la dent féroce de la femme.
Ne cherchez plus mon cœur; les bêtes l'ont mangé.

Mon cœur est un palais flétri par la cohue;
On s'y soûle, on s'y tue, on s'y prend aux cheveux.
 – Un parfum nage autour de votre gorge nue!…

O Beauté, dur fléau des âmes! tu le veux!
Avec tes yeux de feu, brillants comme des fêtes!
Calcine ces lambeaux qu'ont épargnés les bêtes!

THE EYES OF BEAUTY

You are a sky of autumn, pale and rose;
But all the sea of sadness in my blood
Surges, and ebbing, leaves my lips morose,
Salt with the memory of the bitter flood.

In vain your hand glides my faint bosom o'er,
That which you seek, beloved, is desecrate
By woman's tooth and talon; ah, no more
Seek in me for a heart which those dogs ate.

It is a ruin where the jackals rest,
And rend and tear and glut themselves and slay –
A perfume swims about your naked breast!

Beauty, hard scourge of spirits, have your way!
With flame-like eyes that at bright feasts have flared
Burn up these tatters that the beasts have spared!

SONNET D'AUTOMNE

Ils me disent, tes yeux, clairs comme le cristal:
« Pour toi, bizarre amant, quel est donc mon mérite? »
 – Sois charmante et tais-toi! Mon cœur, que tout irrite,
Excepté la candeur de l'antique animal,

Ne veut pas te montrer son secret infernal,
Berceuse dont la main aux longs sommeils m'invite,
Ni sa noire légende avec la flamme écrite.
Je hais la passion et l'esprit me fait mal!

Aimons-nous doucement. L'Amour dans sa guérite,
Ténébreux, embusqué, bande son arc fatal.
Je connais les engins de son vieil arsenal:

Crime, horreur et folie! – O pâle marguerite!
Comme moi n'es-tu pas un soleil automnal,
O ma si blanche, ô ma si froide Marguerite?

SONNET OF AUTUMN

They say to me, thy clear and crystal eyes:
    "Why dost thou love me so, strange lover mine?"
Be sweet, be still! My heart and soul despise
    All save that antique brute-like faith of thine;

And will not bare the secret of their shame
    To thee whose hand soothes me to slumbers long,
Nor their black legend write for thee in flame!
    Passion I hate, a spirit does me wrong.

Let us love gently. Love, from his retreat,
Ambushed and shadowy, bends his fatal bow,
And I too well his ancient arrows know:

Crime, horror, folly. O pale marguerite,
Thou art as I, a bright sun fallen low,
O my so white, my so cold Marguerite.

REMORDS POSTHUME

Lorsque tu dormiras, ma belle ténébreuse,
Au fond d'un monument construit en marbre noir,
Et lorsque tu n'auras pour alcôve et manoir
Qu'un caveau pluvieux et qu'une fosse creuse;

Quand la pierre, opprimant ta poitrine peureuse
Et tes flancs qu'assouplit un charmant nonchaloir,
Empêchera ton cœur de battre et de vouloir,
Et tes pieds de courir leur course aventureuse,

Le tombeau, confident de mon rêve infini,
 – Car le tombeau toujours comprendra le poète, –
Durant ces longues nuits d'où le somme est banni,

Te dira: « Que vous sert, courtisane imparfaite,
De n'avoir pas connu ce que pleurent les morts? »
 – Et le ver rongera ta peau comme un remords.

THE REMORSE OF THE DEAD

O shadowy Beauty mine, when thou shalt sleep
    In the deep heart of a black marble tomb;
When thou for mansion and for bower shalt keep
    Only one rainy cave of hollow gloom;

And when the stone upon thy trembling breast,
    And on thy straight sweet body's supple grace,
Crushes thy will and keeps thy heart at rest,
    And holds those feet from their adventurous race;

Then the deep grave, who shares my reverie,
(For the deep grave is aye the poet's friend)
During long nights when sleep is far from thee,

Shall whisper: "Ah, thou didst not comprehend
The dead wept thus, thou woman frail and weak" –
And like remorse the worm shall gnaw thy cheek.

LE REVENANT

Comme les anges à l'œil fauve,
Je reviendrai dans ton alcôve
Et vers toi glisserai sans bruit
Avec les ombres de la nuit;

Et je te donnerai, ma brune,
Des baisers froids comme la lune
Et des caresses de serpent
Autour d'une fosse rampant.

Quand viendra le matin livide,
Tu trouveras ma place vide,
Où jusqu'au soir il fera froid.

Comme d'autres par la tendresse,
Sur ta vie et sur ta jeunesse,
Moi, je veux régner par l'effroi!

THE GHOST

Softly as brown-eyed Angels rove
I will return to thy alcove.
And glide upon the night to thee,
Treading the shadows silently.

And I will give to thee, my own,
Kisses as icy as the moon,
And the caresses of a snake
Cold gliding in the thorny brake.

And when returns the livid morn
Thou shalt find all my place forlorn
And chilly, till the falling night.

Others would rule by tenderness
Over thy life and youthfulness,
But I would conquer thee by fright!

A UNE MADONE

Ex-voto dans le goût espagnol

Je veux bâtir pour toi, Madone, ma maîtresse,
Un autel souterrain au fond de ma détresse,
Et creuser dans le coin le plus noir de mon cœur,
Loin du désir mondain et du regard moqueur,
Une niche, d'azur et d'or tout émaillée,
Où tu te dresseras, Statue émerveillée.
Avec mes Vers polis, treillis d'un pur métal
Savamment constellé de rimes de cristal
Je ferai pour ta tête une énorme Couronne;
Et dans ma Jalousie, ô mortelle Madone
Je saurai te tailler un Manteau, de façon
Barbare, roide et lourd, et doublé de soupçon,
Qui, comme une guérite, enfermera tes charmes,
Non de Perles brodé, mais de toutes mes Larmes!
Ta Robe, ce sera mon Désir, frémissant,
Onduleux, mon Désir qui monte et qui descend,
Aux pointes se balance, aux vallons se repose,
Et revêt d'un baiser tout ton corps blanc et rose.
Je te ferai de mon Respect de beaux Souliers
De satin, par tes pieds divins humiliés,
Qui, les emprisonnant dans une molle étreinte
Comme un moule fidèle en garderont l'empreinte.
Si je ne puis, malgré tout mon art diligent
Pour Marchepied tailler une Lune d'argent
Je mettrai le Serpent qui me mord les entrailles
Sous tes talons, afin que tu foules et railles
Reine victorieuse et féconde en rachats
Ce monstre tout gonflé de haine et de crachats.
Tu verras mes Pensers, rangés comme les Cierges

Devant l'autel fleuri de la Reine des Vierges
Etoilant de reflets le plafond peint en bleu,
Te regarder toujours avec des yeux de feu;
Et comme tout en moi te chérit et t'admire,
Tout se fera Benjoin, Encens, Oliban, Myrrhe,
Et sans cesse vers toi, sommet blanc et neigeux,
En Vapeurs montera mon Esprit orageux.

Enfin, pour compléter ton rôle de Marie,
Et pour mêler l'amour avec la barbarie,
Volupté noire! des sept Péchés capitaux,
Bourreau plein de remords, je ferai sept Couteaux
Bien affilés, et comme un jongleur insensible,
Prenant le plus profond de ton amour pour cible,
Je les planterai tous dans ton Cœur pantelant,
Dans ton Cœur sanglotant, dans ton Cœur ruisselant!

TO A MADONNA

(*An Ex-Voto in the Spanish taste.*)

Madonna, mistress. I would build for thee
An altar deep in the sad soul of me;
And in the darkest corner of my heart,
From mortal hopes and mocking eyes apart,
Carve of enamelled blue and gold a shrine
For thee to stand erect in, Image divine!
And with a mighty Crown thou shalt be crowned
Wrought of the gold of my smooth Verse, set round
With starry crystal rhymes; and I will make,
O mortal maid, a Mantle for thy sake,
And weave it of my jealousy, a gown
Heavy, barbaric, stiff, and weighted down
With my distrust, and broider round the hem
Not pearls, but all my tears in place of them.
And then thy wavering, trembling robe shall be
All the desires that rise and fall in me
From mountain-peaks to valleys of repose,
Kissing thy lovely body's white and rose.
For thy humiliated feet divine,
Of my Respect I'll make thee Slippers fine
Which, prisoning them within a gentle fold,

Shall keep their imprint like a faithful mould.
And if my art, unwearying and discreet,
Can make no Moon of Silver for thy feet
To have for Footstool, then thy heel shall rest
Upon the snake that gnaws within my breast,
Victorious Queen of whom our hope is born!
And thou shalt trample down and make a scorn

Of the vile reptile swollen up with hate.
And thou shalt see my thoughts, all consecrate,
Like candles set before thy flower-strewn shrine,
O Queen of Virgins, and the taper-shine
Shall glimmer star-like in the vault of blue,
With eyes of flame for ever watching you.
While all the love and worship in my sense
Will be sweet smoke of myrrh and frankincense.
Ceaselessly up to thee, white peak of snow,
My stormy spirit will in vapours go!

And last, to make thy drama all complete,
That love and cruelty may mix and meet,
I, thy remorseful torturer, will take
All the Seven Deadly Sins, and from them make
In darkest joy, Seven Knives, cruel-edged and keen,
And like a juggler choosing, O my Queen,
That spot profound whence love and mercy start,
I'll plunge them all within thy panting heart!

LE COUVERCLE

En quelque lieu qu'il aille, ou sur mer ou sur terre,
Sous un climat de flamme ou sous un soleil blanc,
Serviteur de Jésus, courtisan de Cythère,
Mendiant ténébreux ou Crésus rutilant,

Citadin, campagnard, vagabond, sédentaire,
Que son petit cerveau soit actif ou soit lent,
Partout l'homme subit la terreur du mystère,
Et ne regarde en haut qu'avec un œil tremblant.

En haut, le Ciel! ce mur de caveau qui l'étouffe,
Plafond illuminé pour un opéra bouffe
Où chaque histrion foule un sol ensanglanté,

Terreur du libertin, espoir du fol ermite;
Le Ciel! couvercle noir de la grande marmite
Où bout l'imperceptible et vaste Humanité.

THE SKY

Where'er he be, on water or on land,
    Under pale suns or climes that flames enfold;
One of Christ's own, or of Cythera's band,
    Shadowy beggar or Crœsus rich with gold;

Citizen, peasant, student, tramp; whate'er
    His little brain may be, alive or dead;
Man knows the fear of mystery everywhere,
    And peeps, with trembling glances, overhead.

The heaven above? A strangling cavern wall;
The lighted ceiling of a music-hall
    Where every actor treads a bloody soil –

The hermit's hope; the terror of the sot;
The sky: the black lid of the mighty pot
    Where the vast human generations boil!

SPLEEN

Je suis comme le roi d'un pays pluvieux,
Riche, mais impuissant, jeune et pourtant très vieux,
Qui, de ses précepteurs méprisant les courbettes,
S'ennuie avec ses chiens comme avec d'autres bêtes.
Rien ne peut l'égayer, ni gibier, ni faucon,
Ni son peuple mourant en face du balcon,
Du bouffon favori la grotesque ballade
Ne distrait plus le front de ce cruel malade;
Son lit fleurdelisé se transforme en tombeau,
Et les dames d'atour, pour qui tout prince est beau,
Ne savent plus trouver d'impudique toilette
Pour tirer un souris de ce jeune squelette.
Le savant qui lui fait de l'or n'a jamais pu
De son être extirper l'élément corrompu,
Et dans ces bains de sang qui des Romains nous viennent
Et dont sur leurs vieux jours les puissants se souviennent,
Il n'a su réchauffer ce cadavre hébété
Où coule au lieu de sang l'eau verte du Léthé.

SPLEEN

I'm like some king in whose corrupted veins
Flows aged blood; who rules a land of rains;
Who, young in years, is old in all distress;
Who flees good counsel to find weariness
Among his dogs and playthings, who is stirred
Neither by hunting-hound nor hunting-bird;
Whose weary face emotion moves no more
E'en when his people die before his door.
His favourite Jester's most fantastic wile
Upon that sick, cruel face can raise no smile;
The courtly dames, to whom all kings are good,
Can lighten this young skeleton's dull mood
No more with shameless toilets. In his gloom
Even his lilied bed becomes a tomb.
The sage who takes his gold essays in vain
To purge away the old corrupted strain,
His baths of blood, that in the days of old
The Romans used when their hot blood grew cold,
Will never warm this dead man's bloodless pains,
For green Lethean water fills his veins.

LES HIBOUX

Sous les ifs noirs qui les abritent
Les hiboux se tiennent rangés,
Ainsi que des dieux étrangers,
Dardant leur œil rouge. Ils méditent.

Sans remuer ils se tiendront
Jusqu'à l'heure mélancolique
Où, poussant le soleil oblique,
Les ténèbres s'établiront.

Leur attitude au sage enseigne
Qu'il faut en ce monde qu'il craigne
Le tumulte et le mouvement;

L'homme ivre d'une ombre qui passe
Porte toujours le châtiment
D'avoir voulu changer de place.

THE OWLS

Under the overhanging yews,
The dark owls sit in solemn state.
Like stranger gods; by twos and twos
Their red eyes gleam. They meditate.

Motionless thus they sit and dream
Until that melancholy hour
When, with the sun's last fading gleam,
The nightly shades assume their power.

From their still attitude the wise
Will learn with terror to despise
All tumult, movement, and unrest;

For he who follows every shade,
Carries the memory in his breast,
Of each unhappy journey made.

BIEN LOIN D'ICI

C'est ici la case sacrée
Où cette fille très parée,
Tranquille et toujours préparée.

D'une main éventant ses seins,
Et son coude dans les coussins,
Écoute pleurer les bassins:

C'est la chambre de Dorothée.
— La brise et l'eau chantent au loin
Leur chanson de sanglots heurtée
Pour bercer cette enfant gâtée.

Du haut en bas, avec grand soin,
Sa peau délicate est frottée
D'huile odorante et de benjoin.
— Des fleurs se pâment dans un coin.

BIEN LOIN D'ICI

Here is the chamber consecrate,
Wherein this maiden delicate,
And enigmatically sedate,

Fans herself while the moments creep,
Upon her cushions half-asleep,
And hears the fountains plash and weep.

Dorothy's chamber undefiled.
The winds and waters sing afar
Their song of sighing strange and wild
To lull to sleep the petted child.

From head to foot with subtle care,
Slaves have perfumed her delicate skin
With odorous oils and benzoin.
And flowers faint in a corner there.

LA MUSIQUE

La musique souvent me prend comme une mer !
   Vers ma pâle étoile,
Sous un plafond de brume ou dans un vaste éther,
   Je mets à la voile ;

La poitrine en avant et les poumons gonflés
   Comme de la toile,
J'escalade le dos des flots amoncelés
   Que la nuit me voile ;

Je sens vibrer en moi toutes les passions
   D'un vaisseau qui souffre ;
Le bon vent, la tempête et ses convulsions

   Sur l'immense gouffre
Me bercent. – D'autres fois, calme plat, grand mimoir
   De mon désespoir !

MUSIC

Music doth oft uplift me like a sea
    Towards my planet pale,
Then through dark fogs or heaven's infinity
I lift my wandering sail.

With breast advanced, drinking the winds that flee,
    And through the cordage wail,
I mount the hurrying waves night hides from me
    Beneath her sombre veil.

I feel the tremblings of all passions known
    To ships before the breeze;
Cradled by gentle winds, or tempest-blown

I pass the abysmal seas
    That are, when calm, the mirror level and fair
Of my despair!

RECUEILLEMENT

Sois sage, ô ma Douleur, et tiens-toi plus tranquille,
Tu réclamais le Soir; il descend; le voici:
Une atmosphère obscure enveloppe la ville,
Aux uns portant la paix, aux autres le souci.

Pendant que des mortels la multitude vile,
Sous le fouet du Plaisir, ce bourreau sans merci,
Va cueillir des remords dans la fête servile,
Ma Douleur, donne-moi la main; viens par ici,

Loin d'eux. Vois se pencher les défuntes Années,
Sur les balcons du ciel, en robes surannées;
Surgir du fond des eaux le Regret souriant;

Le Soleil moribond s'endormir sous une arche,
Et, comme un long linceul traînant à l'Orient,
Entends, ma chère, entends la douce Nuit qui marche.

CONTEMPLATION

Thou, O my Grief, be wise and tranquil still,
The eve is thine which even now drops down,
To carry peace or care to human will,
And in a misty veil enfolds the town.

While the vile mortals of the multitude,
By pleasure, cruel tormentor, goaded on,
Gather remorseful blossoms in light mood –
Grief, place thy hand in mine, let us be gone

Far from them. Lo, see how the vanished years,
In robes outworn lean over heaven's rim;
And from the water, smiling through her tears,

Remorse arises, and the sun grows dim;
And in the east, her long shroud trailing light,
List, O my grief, the gentle steps of Night.

A UNE MENDIANTE ROUSSE

Blanche fille aux cheveux roux,
Dont ta robe par ses trous
Laisse voir la pauvreté
   Et la beauté,

Pour moi, poète chétif,
Ton jeune corps maladif
Plein de taches de rousseur
   A sa douceur.

Tu portes plus galamment
Qu'une reine de roman
Ses cothurnes de velours
   Tes sabots lourds.

Au lieu d'un haillon trop court,
Qu'un superbe habit de cour
Traîne à plis bruyants et longs
   Sur tes talons;

Et place de bas troués,
Que pour les yeux des roués
Sur ta jambe un poignard d'or
   Reluise encor;

Que des nœuds mal attachés
Dévoilent pour nos péchés
Tes deux beaux seins, radieux
   Comme des yeux;

Que pour te déshabiller
Tes bras se fassent prier

Et chassent à coups mutins
   Les doigts lutins;

--Perles de la plus belle eau,
Sonnets de maître Belleau
Par tes galants mis aux fers
   Sans cesse offerts,

Valetaille de rimeurs
Te dédiant leurs primeurs
Et contemplant ton soulier
   Sous l'escalier,

Maint page épris du hasard,
Maint seigneur et maint Ronsard
Epieraient pour le déduit
   Ton frais réduit!

Tu compterais dans tes lits
Plus de baisers que de lys
Et rangerais sous tes lois
   Plus d'un Valois!

--Cependant tu vas gueusant
Quelque vieux débris gisant
Au seuil de quelque Véfour
   De carrefour;

Tu vas lorgnant en dessous
Des bijoux de vingt-neuf sous
Dont je ne puis, oh! pardon!
   Te faire don;

Va donc, sans autre ornement,
Parfum, perles, diamant,

Que ta maigre nudité,
 O ma beauté!

TO A BROWN BEGGAR-MAID

White maiden with the russet hair,
Whose garments, through their holes, declare
That poverty is part of you,
    And beauty too.

To me, a sorry bard and mean,
Your youthful beauty, frail and lean,
With summer freckles here and there,
    Is sweet and fair.

Your sabots tread the roads of chance,
And not one queen of old romance
Carried her velvet shoes and lace
    With half your grace.

In place of tatters far too short
Let the proud garments worn at Court
Fall down with rustling fold and pleat
    About your feet;

In place of stockings, worn and old,
Let a keen dagger all of gold
Gleam in your garter for the eyes
    Of roués wise;

Let ribbons carelessly untied
Reveal to us the radiant pride
Of your white bosom purer far
    Than any star;

Let your white arms uncovered shine.
Polished and smooth and half divine;

And let your elfish fingers chase
    With riotous grace

The purest pearls that softly glow.
The sweetest sonnets of Belleau,
Offered by gallants ere they fight
    For your delight;

And many fawning rhymers who
Inscribe their first thin book to you
Will contemplate upon the stair
    Your slipper fair;

And many a page who plays at cards,
And many lords and many bards,
Will watch your going forth, and burn
    For your return;

And you will count before your glass
More kisses than the lily has;
And more than one Valois will sigh
    When you pass by.

But meanwhile you are on the tramp,
Begging your living in the damp,
Wandering mean streets and alleys o'er,
    From door to door;

And shilling bangles in a shop
Cause you with eager eyes to stop,
And I, alas, have not a son
    To give to you.

Then go, with no more ornament,
Pearl, diamond, or subtle scent,

Than your own fragile naked grace
  And lovely face.

LE CYGNE

A VICTOR HUGO

I

Andromaque, je pense à vous! — Ce petit fleuve,
Pauvre et triste miroir où jadis resplendit
L'immense majesté de vos douleurs de veuve,
Ce Simoïs menteur qui par vos pleurs grandit,

A fécondé soudain ma mémoire fertile,
Comme je traversais le nouveau Carrousel.
 — Le vieux Paris n'est plus (la forme d'une ville
Change plus vite, hélas! que le cœur d'un mortel);

Je ne vois qu'en esprit tout ce camp de baraques,
Ces tas de chapiteaux ébauchés et de fûts,
Les herbes, les gros blocs verdis par l'eau des flasques
Et, brillant aux carreaux, le bric-à-brac confus.

Là s'étalait jadis une ménagerie;
Là je vis, un matin, à l'heure où sous les cieux
Clairs et froids le Travail s'éveille, où la voirie
Pousse un sombre ouragan dans l'air silencieux,

Un cygne qui s'était évadé de sa cage,
Et, de ses pieds palmés frottant le pavé sec,
Sur le sol raboteux traînait son grand plumage.
Près d'un ruisseau sans eau la bête ouvrant le bec,

Baignait nerveusement ses ailes dans la poudre,
Et disait, le cœur plein de son beau lac natal:

« Eau, quand donc pleuvras-tu ? quand tonneras-tu,
Je vois ce malheureux, mythe étrange et fatal, foudre ?

Vers le ciel quelquefois, comme l'homme d'Ovide,
Vers le ciel ironique et cruellement bleu,
Sur son cou convulsif tendant sa tête avide,
Comme s'il adressait des reproches à Dieu !

II

Paris change, mais rien dans ma mélancolie
N'a bougé ! palais neufs, échafaudages, blocs,
Vieux faubourgs, tout pour moi devient allégorie,
Et mes chers souvenirs sont plus lourds que des rocs.

Aussi devant ce Louvre une image m'opprime :
Je pense à mon grand cygne, avec ses gestes fous,
Comme les exilés, ridicule et sublime,
Et rongé d'un désir sans trêve ! et puis à vous,

Andromaque, des bras d'un grand époux tombée,
Vil bétail, sous la main du superbe Pyrrhus,
Auprès d'un tombeau vide en extase courbée ;
Veuve d'Hector, hélas ! et femme d'Hélénus !

Je pense à la négresse, amaigrie et phtisique,
Piétinant dans la boue, et cherchant, l'œil hagard,
Les cocotiers absents de la superbe Afrique
Derrière la muraille immense du brouillard ;

A quiconque a perdu ce qui ne se retrouve
Jamais ! jamais ! à ceux qui s'abreuvent de pleurs
Et tettent la Douleur comme une bonne louve !

Aux maigres orphelins séchant comme des fleurs!

Ainsi dans la forêt où mon esprit s'exile
Un vieux Souvenir sonne à plein souffle du cor!
Je pense aux matelots oubliés dans une île,
Aux captifs, aux vaincus!... à bien d'autres encor!

THE SWAN

I

Andromache, I think of you! The stream,
The poor, sad mirror where in bygone days
Shone all the majesty of your widowed grief,
The lying Simoïs flooded by your tears,
Made all my fertile memory blossom forth
As I passed by the new-built Carrousel.
Old Paris is no more (a town, alas,
Changes more quickly than man's heart may change);
Yet in my mind I still can see the booths;
The heaps of brick and rough-hewn capitals;
The grass; the stones all over-green with moss;
The *débris*, and the square-set heaps of tiles.

There a menagerie was once outspread;
And there I saw, one morning at the hour
When toil awakes beneath the cold, clear sky,
And the road roars upon the silent air,
A swan who had escaped his cage, and walked
On the dry pavement with his webby feet,
And trailed his spotless plumage on the ground.

And near a waterless stream the piteous swan
Opened his beak, and bathing in the dust
His nervous wings, he cried (his heart the while
Filled with a vision of his own fair lake):
"O water, when then wilt thou come in rain?
Lightning, when wilt thou glitter?"

                    Sometimes yet
I see the hapless bird – strange, fatal myth –

Like him that Ovid writes of, lifting up
Unto the cruelly blue, ironic heavens,
With stretched, convulsive neck a thirsty face,
As though he sent reproaches up to God!

II

Paris may change; my melancholy is fixed.
New palaces, and scaffoldings, and blocks,
And suburbs old, are symbols all to me
Whose memories are as heavy as a stone.
And so, before the Louvre, to vex my soul,
The image came of my majestic swan
With his mad gestures, foolish and sublime,
As of an exile whom one great desire
Gnaws with no truce. And then I thought of you,
Andromache! torn from your hero's arms;
Beneath the hand of Pyrrhus in his pride;

Bent o'er an empty tomb in ecstasy;
Widow of Hector – wife of Helenus!
And of the negress, wan and phthisical,
Tramping the mud, and with her haggard eyes
Seeking beyond the mighty walls of fog
The absent palm-trees of proud Africa;
Of all who lose that which they never find;
Of all who drink of tears; all whom grey grief
Gives suck to as the kindly wolf gave suck;
Of meagre orphans who like blossoms fade.
And one old Memory like a crying horn
Sounds through the forest where my soul is lost....
I think of sailors on some isle forgotten;
Of captives; vanquished ... and of many more.

LES SEPT VIEILLARDS

A VICTOR HUGO

Fourmillante cité, cité pleine de rêves,
Où le spectre en plein jour raccroche le passant!
Les mystères partout coulent comme des sèves
Dans les canaux étroits du colosse puissant.

Un matin, cependant que dans la triste rue
Les maisons, dont la brume allongeait la hauteur,
Simulaient les deux quais d'une rivière accrue,
Et que, décor semblable à l'âme de l'acteur,

Un brouillard sale et jaune inondait tout l'espace,
Je suivais, roidissant mes nerfs comme un héros
Et discutant avec mon âme déjà lasse,
Le faubourg secoué par les lourds tombereaux.

Tout à coup, un vieillard dont les guenilles jaunes
Imitaient la couleur de ce ciel pluvieux,
Et dont l'aspect aurait fait pleuvoir les aumônes,
Sans la méchanceté qui luisait dans ses yeux,

M'apparut. On eût dit sa prunelle trempée
Dans le fiel; son regard aiguisait les frimas,
Et sa barbe à longs poils, roide comme une épée,
Se projetait, pareille à celle de Judas.

Il n'était pas voûté, mais cassé, son échine
Faisant avec sa jambe un parfait angle droit,
Si bien que son bâton, parachevant sa mine,
Lui donnait la tournure et le pas maladroit

D'un quadrupède infirme ou d'un juif à trois pattes.
Dans la neige et la boue il allait s'empêtrant,
Comme s'il écrasait des morts sous ses savates,
Hostile à l'univers plutôt qu'indifférent.

Son pareil le suivait: barbe, œil, dos, bâton, loques,
Nul trait ne distinguait, du même enfer venu,
Ce jumeau centenaire, et ces spectres baroques
Marchaient du même pas vers un but inconnu.

A quel complot infâme étais-je donc en butte,
Ou quel méchant hasard ainsi m'humiliait?
Car je comptai sept fois, de minute en minute,
Ce sinistre vieillard qui se multipliait!

Que celui-là qui rit de mon inquiétude,
Et qui n'est pas saisi d'un frisson fraternel
Songe bien que malgré tant de décrépitude
Ces sept monstres hideux avaient l'air éternel!

Aurais-je, sans mourir, contemplé le huitième,
Sosie inexorable, ironique et fatal,
Dégoûtant Phénix, fils et père de lui-même?
— Mais je tournai le dos au cortège infernal.

Exaspéré comme un ivrogne qui voit double,
Je rentrai, je fermai ma porte, épouvanté,
Malade et morfondu, l'esprit fiévreux et trouble,
Blessé par le mystère et par l'absurdité!

Vainement ma raison voulait prendre la barre;
La tempête en jouant déroutait ses efforts,
Et mon âme dansait, dansait, vieille gabarre
Sans mâts, sur une mer monstrueuse et sans bords!

THE SEVEN OLD MEN

O swarming city, city full of dreams,
Where in full day the spectre walks and speaks;
Mighty colossus, in your narrow veins
My story flows as flows the rising sap.

One morn, disputing with my tired soul,
And like a hero stiffening all my nerves,
I trod a suburb shaken by the jar
Of rolling wheels, where the fog magnified
The houses either side of that sad street,
So they seemed like two wharves the ebbing flood
Leaves desolate by the river-side. A mist,
Unclean and yellow, inundated space –
A scene that would have pleased an actor's soul.
Then suddenly an aged man, whose rags
Were yellow as the rainy sky, whose looks
Should have brought alms in floods upon his head,
Without the misery gleaming in his eye,
Appeared before me; and his pupils seemed
To have been washed with gall; the bitter frost
Sharpened his glance; and from his chin a beard
Sword-stiff and ragged, Judas-like stuck forth.
He was not bent but broken: his backbone
Made a so true right angle with his legs,
That, as he walked, the tapping stick which gave
The finish to the picture, made him seem
Like some infirm and stumbling quadruped
Or a three-legged Jew. Through snow and mud
He walked with troubled and uncertain gait,
As though his sabots trod upon the dead,
Indifferent and hostile to the world.

His double followed him: tatters and stick
And back and eye and beard, all were the same;
Out of the same Hell, indistinguishable,
These centenarian twins, these spectres odd,
Trod the same pace toward some end unknown.
To what fell complot was I then exposed!
Humiliated by what evil chance?
For as the minutes one by one went by
Seven times I saw this sinister old man
Repeat his image there before my eyes!

Let him who smiles at my inquietude,
Who never trembled at a fear like mine,
Know that in their decrepitude's despite
These seven old hideous monsters had the mien
Of beings immortal.

            Then, I thought, must I,
Undying, contemplate the awful eighth;
Inexorable, fatal, and ironic double;
Disgusting Phoenix, father of himself
And his own son! In terror then I turned
My back upon the infernal band, and fled
To my own place, and closed my door; distraught
And like a drunkard who sees all things twice,
With feverish troubled spirit, chilly and sick,
Wounded by mystery and absurdity!

In vain my reason tried to cross the bar,
The whirling storm but drove her back again;
And my soul tossed, and tossed, an outworn wreck,
Mastless, upon a monstrous, shoreless sea.

LES PETITES VIEILLES

A VICTOR HUGO

I

Dans les plis sinueux des vieilles capitales,
Où tout, même l'horreur, tourne aux enchantements,
Je guette, obéissant à mes humeurs fatales,
Des êtres singuliers, décrépits et charmants.

Ces monstres disloqués furent jadis des femmes,
Eponine ou Laïs!--Monstres brisés, bossus
Ou tordus, aimons-les! ce sont encor des âmes.
Sous des jupons troués et sous de froids tissus

Ils rampent, flagellés par les bises iniques,
Frémissant au fracas roulant des omnibus,
Et serrant sur leur flanc, ainsi que des reliques,
Un petit sac brodé de fleurs ou de rébus;

Ils trottent, tout pareils à des marionnettes;
Se traînent, comme font les animaux blessés,
Ou dansent, sans vouloir danser, pauvres sonnettes
Où se pend un Démon sans pitié! Tout cassés

Qu'ils sont, ils ont des yeux perçants comme une vrille,
Luisants comme ces trous où l'eau dort dans la nuit;
Ils ont les yeux divins de la petite fille
Qui s'étonne et qui rit à tout ce qui reluit.

--Avez-vous observé que maints cercueils de vieilles
Sont presque aussi petits que celui d'un enfant?

La Mort savante met dans ces bières pareilles
Un symbole d'un goût bizarre et captivant,

Et lorsque j'entrevois un fantôme débile
Traversant de Paris le fourmillant tableau,
Il me semble toujours que cet être fragile
S'en va tout doucement vers un nouveau berceau;

A moins que, méditant sur la géométrie,
Je ne cherche, à l'aspect de ces membres discords,
Combien de fois il faut que l'ouvrier varie
La forme de la boîte où l'on met tous ces corps.

--Ces yeux sont des puits faits d'un million de larmes,
Des creusets qu'un métal refroidi pailleta...
Ces yeux mystérieux ont d'invincibles charmes
Pour celui que l'austère Infortune allaita!

II

De l'ancien Frascati Vestale énamourée;
Prêtresse de Thalie, hélas! dont le souffleur
Défunt, seul, sait le nom; célèbre évaporée
Que Tivoli jadis ombragea dans sa fleur,

Toutes m'enivrent! mais parmi ces êtres frêles
Il en est qui, faisant de la douleur un miel,
Ont dit au Dévouement qui leur prêtait ses ailes:
« Hippogriffe puissant, mène-moi jusqu'au ciel! »

L'une, par sa patrie au malheur exercée,
L'autre, que son époux surchargea de douleurs,
L'autre, par son enfant Madone transpercée,
Toutes auraient pu faire un fleuve avec leurs pleurs!

III

Ah! que j'en ai suivi, de ces petites vieilles!
Une, entre autres, à l'heure où le soleil tombant
Ensanglante le ciel de blessures vermeilles,
Pensive, s'asseyait à l'écart sur un banc,

Pour entendre un de ces concerts, riches de cuivre,
Dont les soldats parfois inondent nos jardins,
Et qui, dans ces soirs dor où l'on se sent revivre,
Versent quelque héroïsme au cœur des citadins.

Celle-là droite encor, fière et sentant la règle,
Humait avidement ce chant vif et guerrier;
Son œil parfois s'ouvrait comme l'œil d'un vieil aigle;
Son front de marbre avait l'air fait pour le laurier!

IV

Telles vous cheminez, stoïques et sans plaintes,
A travers le chaos des vivantes cités,
Mères au cœur saignant, courtisanes ou saintes,
Dont autrefois les noms par tous étaient cités.

Vous qui fûtes la grâce ou qui fûtes la gloire,
Nul ne vous reconnaît! un ivrogne incivil
Vous insulte en passant d'un amour dérisoire;
Sur vos talons gambade un enfant lâche et vil.

Honteuses d'exister, ombres ratatinées,
Peureuses, le dos bas, vous côtoyer les murs,
Et nul ne vous salue, étranges destinées!
Débris d'humanité pour l'éternité mûrs!

Mais moi, moi qui de loin tendrement vous surveille,
L'œil inquiet, fixé sur vos pas incertains,
Tout comme si j'étais votre père, ô merveille!
Je goûte à votre insu des plaisirs clandestins:

Je vois s'épanouir vos passions novices;
Sombres ou lumineux, je vis vos jours perdus;
Mon cœur multiplié jouit de tous vos vices!
Mon âme resplendit de toutes vos vertus!

Ruines! ma famille! ô cerveaux congénères!
Je vous fais chaque soir un solennel adieu!
Où serez-vous demain, Eves octogénaires,
Sur qui pèse la griffe effroyable de Dieu?

THE LITTLE OLD WOMEN

I

Deep in the tortuous folds of ancient towns,
Where all, even horror, to enchantment turns,
I watch, obedient to my fatal mood,
For the decrepit, strange and charming beings,
The dislocated monsters that of old
Were lovely women – Laïs or Eponine!
Hunchbacked and broken, crooked though they be,
Let us still love them, for they still have souls.
They creep along wrapped in their chilly rags,
Beneath the whipping of the wicked wind,
They tremble when an omnibus rolls by,
And at their sides, a relic of the past,
A little flower-embroidered satchel hangs.
They trot about, most like to marionettes;
They drag themselves, as does a wounded beast;
Or dance unwillingly as a clapping bell
Where hangs and swings a demon without pity.
Though they be broken they have piercing eyes,
That shine like pools where water sleeps at night;
The astonished and divine eyes of a child
Who laughs at all that glitters in the world.
Have you not seen that most old women's shrouds
Are little like the shroud of a dead child?
Wise Death, in token of his happy whim,
Wraps old and young in one enfolding sheet.
And when I see a phantom, frail and wan,
Traverse the swarming picture that is Paris,
It ever seems as though the delicate thing
Trod with soft steps towards a cradle new.
And then I wonder, seeing the twisted form,

How many times must workmen change the shape
Of boxes where at length such limbs are laid?
These eyes are wells brimmed with a million tears;
Crucibles where the cooling metal pales –
Mysterious eyes that are strong charms to him
Whose life-long nurse has been austere Disaster.

II

The love-sick vestal of the old "Frasciti";
Priestess of Thalia, alas! whose name
Only the prompter knows and he is dead;
Bygone celebrities that in bygone days
The Tivoli o'ershadowed in their bloom;
All charm me; yet among these beings frail
Three, turning pain to honey-sweetness, said
To the Devotion that had lent them wings:
"Lift me, O powerful Hippogriffe, to the skies" –
One by her country to despair was driven;
One by her husband overwhelmed with grief;
One wounded by her child, Madonna-like;
Each could have made a river with her tears.

III

Oft have I followed one of these old women,
One among others, when the falling sun
Reddened the heavens with a crimson wound –
Pensive, apart, she rested on a bench
To hear the brazen music of the band,
Played by the soldiers in the public park
To pour some courage into citizens' hearts,
On golden eves when all the world revives.

Proud and erect she drank the music in,
The lively and the warlike call to arms;
Her eyes blinked like an ancient eagle's eyes;
Her forehead seemed to await the laurel crown!

IV

Thus you do wander, uncomplaining Stoics,
Through all the chaos of the living town:
Mothers with bleeding hearts, saints, courtesans,
Whose names of yore were on the lips of all;
Who were all glory and all grace, and now
None know you; and the brutish drunkard stops,
Insulting you with his derisive love;
And cowardly urchins call behind your back.
Ashamed of living, withered shadows all,
With fear-bowed backs you creep beside the walls,
And none salute you, destined to loneliness!
Refuse of Time ripe for Eternity!
But I, who watch you tenderly afar,
With unquiet eyes on your uncertain steps,
As though I were your father, I – O wonder! –
Unknown to you taste secret, hidden joy.
I see your maiden passions bud and bloom,
Sombre or luminous, and your lost days
Unroll before me while my heart enjoys
All your old vices, and my soul expands
To all the virtues that have once been yours.
Ruined! and my sisters! O congenerate hearts,
Octogenarian Eves o'er whom is stretched
God's awful claw, where will you be to-morrow?

MADRIGAL TRISTE

Que m'importe que tu sois sage?
Sois belle! et sois triste! Les pleurs
Ajoutent un charme au visage,
Comme le fleuve au paysage;
L'orage rajeunit les fleurs.

Je t'aime surtout quand la joie
S'enfuit de ton front terrassé;
Quand ton cœur dans l'horreur se noie;
Quand sur ton présent se déploie
Le nuage affreux du passé.

Je t'aime quand ton grand œil verse
Une eau chaude comme le sang;
Quand, malgré ma main qui te berce,
Ton angoisse, trop lourde, perce
Comme un râle d'agonisant.
J'aspire, volupté divine!

Hymne profond, délicieux!
Tous les sanglots de ta poitrine,
Et crois que ton cœur s'illumine
Des perles que versent tes yeux!

Je sais que ton cœur, qui regorge
De vieux amours déracinés,
Flamboie encor comme une forge,
Et que tu couves sous ta gorge
Un peu de l'orgueil des damnés;

Mais tant, ma chère, que tes rêves
N'auront pas reflété l'Enfer,

Et qu'en un cauchemar sans trêves,
Songeant de poisons et de glaives,
Eprise de poudre et de fer,

N'ouvrant à chacun qu'avec crainte,
Déchiffrant le malheur partout,
Te convulsant quand l'heure tinte,
Tu n'auras pas senti l'étreinte
De l'irrésistible Dégoût,

Tu ne pourras, esclave reine
Qui ne m'aimes qu'avec effroi,
Dans l'horreur de la nuit malsaine
Me dire, l'âme de cris pleine:
« Je suis ton égale, ô mon Roi! »

A MADRIGAL OF SORROW

What do I care though you be wise?
    Be sad, be beautiful; your tears
But add one more charm to your eyes,
As streams to valleys where they rise;
    And fairer every flower appears

After the storm. I love you most
    When joy has fled your brow downcast;
When your heart is in horror lost,
And o'er your present like a ghost
    Floats the dark shadow of the past.

I love you when the teardrop flows,
    Hotter than blood, from your large eye;
When I would hush you to repose
Your heavy pain breaks forth and grows
    Into a loud and tortured cry.

And then, voluptuousness divine!
    Delicious ritual and profound!
I drink in every sob like wine,
And dream that in your deep heart shine
    The pearls wherein your eyes were drowned.

I know your heart, which overflows
    With outworn loves long cast aside,
Still like a furnace flames and glows,
And you within your breast enclose
    A damnèd soul's unbending pride;

But till your dreams without release
    Reflect the leaping flames of hell;

Till in a nightmare without cease
You dream of poison to bring peace,
    And love cold steel and powder well;

And tremble at each opened door,
    And feel for every man distrust,
And shudder at the striking hour –
Till then you have not felt the power
    Of Irresistible Disgust.

My queen, my slave, whose love is fear,
    When you awaken shuddering,
Until that awful hour be here,
You cannot say at midnight drear:
    "I am your equal, O my King!"

L'IDEAL

Ce ne seront jamais ces beautés de vignettes,
Produits avariés, nés d'un siècle vaurien,
Ces pieds à brodequins, ces doigts à castagnettes,
Qui sauront satisfaire un cœur comme le mien.

Je laisse, à Gavarni, poète des chloroses,
Soa troupeau gazouillant de beautés d'hôpital,
Car je ne puis trouver parmi ces pâles roses
Une fleur qui ressemble à mon rouge idéal.

Ce qu'il faut à ce cœur profond comme un abîme,
C'est vous, Lady Macbeth, âme puissante au crime,
Rêve d'Eschyle éclos au climat des autans;

Ou bien toi, grand Nuit, fille de Michel-Ange,
Qui tors paisiblement dans une pose étrange
Tes appas façonnés aux bouches des Titans!

THE IDEAL

Not all the beauties in old prints vignetted,
    The worthless products of an outworn age,
With slippered feet and fingers castanetted,
    The thirst of hearts like this heart can assuage.

To Gavarni, the poet of chloroses,
    I leave his troupes of beauties sick and wan;
I cannot find among these pale, pale roses,
    The red ideal mine eyes would gaze upon.

Lady Macbeth, the lovely star of crime,
    The Greek poet's dream born in a northern clime –
Ah, she could quench my dark heart's deep desiring;

Or Michelangelo's dark daughter Night,
    In a strange posture dreamily admiring
Her beauty fashioned for a giant's delight!

BRUMES ET PLUIES

O fins d'automne, hivers, printemps trempés de boue,
Endormeuses saisons! je vous aime et vous loue
D'envelopper ainsi mon cœur et mon cerveau
D'un linceul vaporeux et d'un vague tombeau.

Dans cette grande plaine où l'autan froid se joue,
Où par les longues nuits la girouette s'enroue,
Mon âme mieux qu'au temps du tiède renouveau
Ouvrira largement ses ailes de corbeau.

Rien n'est plus doux au cœur plein de choses funèbres,
Et sur qui dès longtemps descendent les frimas,
O blafardes saisons, reines de nos climats!

Que l'aspect permanent de vos pâles ténèbres,
 – Si ce n'est par un soir sans lune, deux à deux,
D'endormir la douleur sur un lit hasardeux.

MIST AND RAIN

Autumns and winters, springs of mire and rain,
Seasons of sleep, I sing your praises loud,
For thus I love to wrap my heart and brain
In some dim tomb beneath a vapoury shroud

In the wide plain where revels the cold wind,
Through long nights when the weathercock whirls round,
More free than in warm summer day my mind
Lifts wide her raven pinions from the ground.

Unto a heart filled with funereal things
That since old days hoar frosts have gathered on,
Naught is more sweet, O pallid, queenly springs,

Than the long pageant of your shadows wan,
Unless it be on moonless eves to weep
On some chance bed and rock our griefs to sleep.

LE COUCHER DU SOLEIL ROMANTIQUE

Que le Soleil est beau quand tout frais il se lève,
Comme une explosion nous lançant son bonjour!
 – Bienheureux celui-là qui peut avec amour
Saluer son coucher plus glorieux qu'un rêve!

Je me souviens!... J'ai vu tout, fleur, source, sillon,
Se pâmer sous son œil comme un cœur qui palpite,..
 – Courons vers l'horizon, il est tard, courons vite,
Pour attraper au moins un oblique rayon!

Mais je poursuis en vain le Dieu qui se retire;
L'irrésistible Nuit établit son empire,
Noire, humide, funeste et pleine de frissons;

Une odeur de tombeau dans les ténèbres nage,
Et mon pied peureux froisse, au bord du marécage,
Des crapauds imprévus et de froids limaçons.

SUNSET

Fair is the sun when first he flames above,
   Flinging his joy down in a happy beam;
And happy he who can salute with love
   The sunset far more glorious than a dream.

Flower, stream, and furrow! – I have seen them all
   In the sun's eye swoon like one trembling heart –
Though it be late let us with speed depart
   To catch at least one last ray ere it fall!

But I pursue the fading god in vain,
For conquering Night makes firm her dark domain,
   Mist and gloom fall, and terrors glide between,

And graveyard odours in the shadow swim,
And my faint footsteps on the marsh's rim,
   Bruise the cold snail and crawling toad unseen.

UNE CHAROGNE

Rappelez-vous l'objet que nous vîmes, mon âme,
    Ce beau matin d'été si doux:
Au détour d'un sentier une charogne infâme
    Sur un lit semé de cailloux,

Les jambes en l'air, comme une femme lubrique,
    Brûlante et suant les poisons,
Ouvrait d'une façon nonchalante et cynique
    Son ventre plein d'exhalaisons.

Le soleil rayonnait sur cette pourriture,
    Comme afin de la cuire à point,
Et de rendre au centuple à la grande Nature
    Tout ce qu'ensemble elle avait joint.

Et le ciel regardait la carcasse superbe
    Comme une fleur s'épanouir;
La puanteur était si forte que sur l'herbe
    Vous crûtes vous évanouir.

Les mouches bourdonnaient sur ce ventre putride,
    D'où sortaient de noirs bataillons
De larves qui coulaient comme un épais liquide
    Le long de ces vivants haillons.

Tout cela descendait, montait comme une vague,
    Où s'élançait en pétillant;
On eût dit que le corps, enflé d'un souffle vague,
    Vivait en se multipliant.

Et ce monde rendait une étrange musique
    Comme l'eau courante et le vent,

Ou le grain qu'un vanneur d'un mouvement rythmique
   Agite et tourne dans son van.

Les formes s'effaçaient et n'étaient plus qu'un rêve,
   Une ébauche lente à venir
Sur la toile oubliée, et que l'artiste achève
   Seulement par le souvenir.

Derrière les rochers une chienne inquiète
   Nous regardait d'un œil fâché,
Epiant le moment de reprendre au squelette
   Le morceau qu'elle avait lâché.

— Et pourtant vous serez semblable à cette ordure,
   A cette horrible infection,
Etoile de mes yeux, soleil de ma nature,
   Vous, mon ange et ma passion!

Oui! telle vous serez, ô la reine des grâces,
   Après les derniers sacrements,
Quand vous irez sous l'herbe et les floraisons grasses,
   Moisir parmi les ossements.

Alors, ô ma beauté, dites à la vermine
   Qui vous mangera de baisers,
Que j'ai gardé la forme et l'essence divine
   De mes amours décomposés!

THE CORPSE

Remember, my Beloved, what thing we met
    By the roadside on that sweet summer day;
There on a grassy couch with pebbles set,
    A loathsome body lay.

The wanton limbs stiff-stretched into the air,
    Steaming with exhalations vile and dank,
In ruthless cynic fashion had laid bare
    The swollen side and flank.

On this decay the sun shone hot from heaven
    As though with chemic heat to broil and burn,
And unto Nature all that she had given
    A hundredfold return.

The sky smiled down upon the horror there
    As on a flower that opens to the day;
So awful an infection smote the air,
    Almost you swooned away.

The swarming flies hummed on the putrid side,
    Whence poured the maggots in a darkling stream,
That ran along these tatters of life's pride
    With a liquescent gleam.

And like a wave the maggots rose and fell,
    The murmuring flies swirled round in busy strife:
It seemed as though a vague breath came to swell
    And multiply with life

The hideous corpse. From all this living world
    A music as of wind and water ran,

Or as of grain in rhythmic motion swirled
 By the swift winnower's fan.

And then the vague forms like a dream died out,
 Or like some distant scene that slowly falls
Upon the artist's canvas, that with doubt
 He only half recalls.

A homeless dog behind the boulders lay
 And watched us both with angry eyes forlorn,
Waiting a chance to come and take away
 The morsel she had torn.

And you, even you, will be like this drear thing,
 A vile infection man may not endure;
Star that I yearn to! Sun that lights my spring!
 O passionate and pure!

Yes, such will you be, Queen of every grace!
 When the last sacramental words are said;
And beneath grass and flowers that lovely face
 Moulders among the dead.

Then, O Beloved, whisper to the worm
 That crawls up to devour you with a kiss,
That I still guard in memory the dear form
 Of love that comes to this!

ALLEGORIE

C'est une femme belle et de riche encolure,
Qui laisse dans son vin traîner sa chevelure.
Les griffes de l'amour, les poisons du tripot,
Tout glisse et tout s'émousse au granit de sa peau.
Elle rit à la Mort et nargue la Débauche,
Ces monstres dont la main, qui toujours gratte et fauche,
Dans ses jeux destructeurs a pourtant respecté
De ce corps ferme et droit la rude majesté.
Elle marche en déesse et repose en sultane;
Elle a dans le plaisir la foi mahométane,
Et dans ses bras ouverts que remplissent ses seins,
Elle appelle des yeux la race des humains.
Elle croit, elle sait, cette vierge inféconde
Et pourtant nécessaire à la marche du monde,
Que la beauté du corps est un sublime don
Qui de toute infamie arrache le pardon;
Elle ignore l'Enfer comme le Purgatoire,
Et, quand l'heure viendra d'entrer dans la Nuit noire,
Elle regardera la face de la Mort,
Ainsi qu'un nouveau-né, — sans haine et sans remord.

AN ALLEGORY

Here is a woman, richly clad and fair,
Who in her wine dips her long, heavy hair;
Love's claws, and that sharp poison which is sin,
Are dulled against the granite of her skin.
Death she defies, Debauch she smiles upon,
For their sharp scythe-like talons every one
Pass by her in their all-destructive play;
Leaving her beauty till a later day.
Goddess she walks; sultana in her leisure;
She has Mohammed's faith that heaven is pleasure,
And bids all men forget the world's alarms
Upon her breast, between her open arms.
She knows, and she believes, this sterile maid,
Without whom the world's onward dream would fade,
That bodily beauty is the supreme gift
Which may from every sin the terror lift.
Hell she ignores, and Purgatory defies;
And when black Night shall roll before her eyes,
She will look straight in Death's grim face forlorn,
Without remorse or hate – as one new born.

FEMMES DAMNEES

Comme un bétail pensif sur le sable couchées,
Elles tournent leurs yeux vers l'horizon des mers,
Et leurs pieds se cherchant et leurs mains rapprochées
Ont de douces langueurs et des frissons amers:

Les unes, cœurs épris des longues confidences,
Dans le fond des bosquets où jasent les ruisseaux,
Vont épelant l'amour des craintives enfances
Et creusent le bois vert des jeunes arbrisseaux;

D'autres, comme des sœurs, marchent lentes et graves
A travers les rochers pleins d'apparitions,
Où saint Antoine a vu surgir comme des laves
Les seins nus et pourprés de ses tentations;

Il en est, aux lueurs des résines croulantes,
Qui dans le creux muet des vieux antres païens
T'appellent au secours de leurs fièvres hurlantes,
O Bacchus, endormeur des remords anciens!

Et d'autres, dont la gorge aime les scapulaires,
Qui, recelant un fouet sous leurs longs vêtements,
Mêlent dans le bois sombre et les nuits solitaires
L'écume du plaisir aux larmes des tourments.

O vierges, ô démons, ô monstres, ô martyres,
De la réalité grands esprits contempteurs,
Chercheuses d'infini, dévotes et satyres,
Tantôt pleines de cris, tantôt pleines de pleurs,

Vous que dans votre enfer mon âme a poursuivies,
Pauvres sœurs, je vous aime autant que je vous plains,

Pour vos mornes douleurs, vos soifs inassouvies,
Et les urnes d'amour dont vos grands cœurs sont pleins!

THE ACCURSED

Like pensive herds at rest upon the sands,
    These to the sea-horizons turn their eyes;
Out of their folded feet and clinging hands
    Bitter sharp tremblings and soft languors rise.

Some tread the thicket by the babbling stream,
    Their hearts with untold secrets ill at ease;
Calling the lover of their childhood's dream,
    They wound the green bark of the shooting trees.

Others like sisters wander, grave and slow,
    Among the rocks haunted by spectres thin,
Where Antony saw as larvæ surge and flow
    The veined bare breasts that tempted him to sin.

Some, when the resinous torch of burning wood
    Flares in lost pagan caverns dark and deep,
Call thee to quench the fever in their blood,
    Bacchus, who singest old remorse to sleep!

Then there are those the scapular bedights,
    Whose long white vestments hide the whip's red stain,
Who mix, in sombre woods on lonely nights,
    The foam of pleasure with the tears of pain.

O virgins, demons, monsters, martyrs! ye
    Who scorn whatever actual appears;
Saints, satyrs, seekers of Infinity,
    So full of cries, so full of bitter tears;

Te whom my soul has followed into hell,
    I love and pity, O sad sisters mine,

Tour thirsts unquenched, your pains no tongue can tell,
And your great hearts, those urns of love divine!

LA BÉATRICE

Dans des terrains cendreux, calcinés, sans verdure,
Comme je me plaignais un jour à la nature,
Et que de ma pensée, en vaguant au hasard,
J'aiguisais lentement sur mon cœur le poignard,
Je vis en plein midi descendre sur ma tête
Un nuage funèbre et gros d'une tempête,
Qui portait un troupeau de démons vicieux,
Semblables à des nains cruels et curieux.
A me considérer froidement ils se mirent,
Et, comme des passants sur un fou qu'ils admirent,
Je les entendis rire et chuchoter entre eux,
En échangeant maint signe et maint clignement d'yeux:

– "Contemplons à loisir cette caricature
Et cette ombre d'Hamlet imitant sa posture,
Le regard indécis et les cheveux au vent.
N'est-ce pas grand'pitié de voir ce bon vivant,
Ce gueux, cet histrion en vacances, ce drôle,
Parce qu'il sait jouer artistement son rôle,
Vouloir intéresser au chant de ses douleurs
Les aigles, les grillons, les ruisseaux et les fleurs,
Et même à nous, auteurs de ces vieilles rubriques,
Réciter en hurlant ses tirades publiques?"

J'aurais pu (mon orgueil aussi haut que les monts
Domine la nuée et le cri des démons)
Détourner simplement ma tête souveraine,
Si je n'eusse pas vu parmi leur troupe obscène,
Crime qui n'a pas fait chanceler le soleil!
La reine de mon cœur au regard nonpareil
Qui riait avec eux de ma sombre détresse
Et leur versait parfois quelque sale caresse.

LA BEATRICE

In a burnt, ashen land, where no herb grew,
I to the winds my cries of anguish threw;
And in my thoughts, in that sad place apart,
Pricked gently with the poignard o'er my heart.
Then in full noon above my head a cloud
Descended tempest-swollen, and a crowd
Of wild, lascivious spirits huddled there,
The cruel and curious demons of the air,
Who coldly to consider me began;
Then, as a crowd jeers some unhappy man,
Exchanging gestures, winking with their eyes –
I heard a laughing and a whispering rise:

"Let us at leisure contemplate this clown,
This shadow of Hamlet aping Hamlet's frown,
With wandering eyes and hair upon the wind.
Is't not a pity that this empty mind,
This tramp, this actor out of work, this droll,
Because he knows how to assume a rôle
Should dream that eagles and insects, streams and woods,
Stand still to hear him chaunt his dolorous moods?

Even unto us, who made these ancient things,
The fool his public lamentation sings."

With pride as lofty as the towering cloud,
I would have stilled these clamouring demons loud,
And turned in scorn my sovereign head away
Had I not seen – O sight to dim the day! –
There in the middle of the troupe obscene
The proud and peerless beauty of my Queen!
She laughed with them at all my dark distress,
And gave to each in turn a vile caress.

L'AME DU VIN

Un soir, l'âme du vin chantait dans les bouteilles:
« Homme, vers toi je pousse, ô cher déshérité,
Sous ma prison de verre et mes cires vermeilles,
Un chant plein de lumière et de fraternité!

Je sais combien il faut, sur la colline en flamme,
De peine, de sueur et de soleil cuisant
Pour engendrer ma vie et pour me donner l'âme;
Mais je ne serai point ingrat ni malfaisant,

Car j'éprouve une joie immense quand je tombe
Dans le gosier d'un homme usé par ses travaux,
Et sa chaude poitrine est une douce tombe
Où je me plais bien mieux que dans mes froids caveaux.

Entends-tu retentir les refrains des dimanches
Et l'espoir qui gazouille en mon sein palpitant?
Les coudes sur la table et retroussant tes manches,
Tu me glorifieras et tu seras content:

J'allumerai les yeux de ta femme ravie;
A ton fils je rendrai sa force et ses couleurs
Et serai pour ce frêle athlète de la vie
L'huile qui raffermit les muscles des lutteurs.

En toi je tomberai, végétale ambroisie,
Grain précieux jeté par l'éternel Semeur,
Pour que de notre amour naisse la poésie
Qui jaillira vers Dieu comme une rare fleur! »

THE SOUL OF WINE

One eve in the bottle sang the soul of wine:
    "Man, unto thee, dear disinherited,
I sing a song of love and light divine –
    Prisoned in glass beneath my seals of red.

"I know thou labourest on the hill of fire,
    In sweat and pain beneath a flaming sun,
To give the life and soul my vines desire,
    And I am grateful for thy labours done.

"For I find joys unnumbered when I lave
    The throat of man by travail long outworn,
And his hot bosom is a sweeter grave
    Of sounder sleep than my cold caves forlorn.

"Hearest thou not the echoing Sabbath sound?
    The hope that whispers in my trembling breast?
Thy elbows on the table! gaze around;
    Glorify me with joy and be at rest.

"To thy wife's eyes I'll bring their long-lost gleam,
    I'll bring back to thy child his strength and light,
To him, life's fragile athlete I will seem
    Rare oil that firms his muscles for the fight.

"I flow in man's heart as ambrosia flows;
    The grain the eternal Sower casts in the sod –
From our first loves the first fair verse arose,
    Flower-like aspiring to the heavens and God!"

LE VIN DES AMANTS

Aujourd'hui l'espace est splendide!
Sans mors, sans éperons, sans bride,
Partons à cheval sur le vin
Pour un ciel féerique et divin!

Comme deux anges que torture
Une implacable calenture,
Dans le bleu cristal du matin
Suivons le mirage lointain!

Mollement balancés sur l'aile
Du tourbillon intelligent,
Dans un délire parallèle,

Ma soeur, côte à côte nageant,
Nous fuirons sans repos ni trêves
Vers le paradis de mes rêves!

THE WINE OF LOVERS

Space rolls to-day her splendour round!
Unbridled, spurless, without bound,
Mount we upon the wings of wine
For skies fantastic and divine!

Let us, like angels tortured by
Some wild delirious phantasy,
Follow the far-off mirage born
In the blue crystal of the morn.

And gently balanced on the wing
Of the wild whirlwind we will ride,
Rejoicing with the joyous thing.

My sister, floating side by side,
Fly we unceasing whither gleams
The distant heaven of my dreams.

LA MORT DES AMANTS

Nous aurons des lits pleins d'odeurs légères,
Des divans profonds comme des tombeaux,
Et d'étranges fleurs sur des étagères,
Ecloses pour nous sous des cieux plus beaux.

Usant à l'envi leurs chaleurs dernières,
Nos deux cœurs seront deux vastes flambeaux,
Qui réfléchiront leurs doubles lumières
Dans nos deux esprits, ces miroirs jumeaux.

Un soir fait de rose et de bleu mystique,
Nous échangerons un éclair unique,
Comme un long sanglot, tout chargé d'adieux ;

Et plus tard un Ange, entr'ouvrant les portes,
Viendra ranimer, fidèle et joyeux,
Les miroirs ternis et les flammes mortes.

THE DEATH OF LOVERS

There shall be couches whence faint odours rise,
    Divans like sepulchres, deep and profound;
Strange flowers that bloomed beneath diviner skies
    The death-bed of our love shall breathe around.

And guarding their last embers till the end,
    Our hearts shall be the torches of the shrine,
And their two leaping flames shall fade and blend
    In the twin mirrors of your soul and mine.

And through the eve of rose and mystic blue
A beam of love shall pass from me to you,
Like a long sigh charged with a last farewell;

And later still an angel, flinging wide
The gates, shall bring to life with joyful spell
The tarnished mirrors and the flames that died.

LA MORT DES PAUVRES

C'est la Mort qui console, hélas! et qui fait vivre;
C'est le but de la vie, et c'est le seul espoir
Qui, comme un élixir, nous monte et nous enivre,
Et nous donne le cœur de marcher jusqu'au soir;

A travers la tempête, et la neige et le givre,
C'est la clarté vibrante à notre horizon noir;
C'est l'auberge fameuse inscrite sur le livre,
Où l'on pourra manger, et dormir, et s'asseoir;

C'est un Ange qui tient dans ses doigts magnétiques
Le sommeil et le don des rêves extatiques,
Et qui refait le lit des gens pauvres et nus;

C'est la gloire des Dieux, c'est le grenier mystique,
C'est la bourse du pauvre et sa patrie antique,
C'est le portique ouvert sur les Cieux inconnus!

THE DEATH OF THE POOR

Death is consoler and Death brings to life;
    The end of all, the solitary hope;
We, drunk with Death's elixir, face the strife,
    Take heart, and mount till eve the weary slope.

Across the storm, the hoar-frost, and the snow,
    Death on our dark horizon pulses clear;
Death is the famous hostel we all know,
    Where we may rest and sleep and have good cheer.

Death is an angel whose magnetic palms
Bring dreams of ecstasy and slumberous calms
To smooth the beds of naked men and poor.

Death is the mystic granary of God;
The poor man's purse; his fatherland of yore;
The Gate that opens into heavens un trod!

BENEDICTION

Lorsque, par un décret des puissances suprêmes,
Le Poète apparaît en ce monde ennuyé,
Sa mère épouvantée et pleine de blasphèmes
Crispe ses poings vers Dieu, qui la prend en pitié:

« Ah! que n'ai-je mis bas tout un nœud de vipères,
Plutôt que de nourrir cette dérision!
Maudite soit la nuit aux plaisirs éphémères
Où mon ventre a conçu mon expiation!

« Puisque tu m'as choisie entre toutes les femmes
Pour être le dégoût de mon triste mari,
Et que je ne puis pas rejeter dans les flammes,
Comme un billet d'amour, ce monstre rabougri,

« Je ferai rejaillir la haine qui m'accable
Sur l'instrument maudit de tes méchancetés,
Et je tordrai si bien cet arbre misérable,
Qu'il ne pourra poussa ses boutons empestés! »

Elle ravale ainsi l'écume de sa haine,
Et, ne comprenant pas les desseins éternels,
Elle-même prépare au fond de la Géhenne
Les bûchers consacrés aux crimes maternels.

Pourtant, sous la tutelle invisible d'un Ange,
L'Enfant déshérité s'enivre de soleil,
Et dans tout ce qu'il boit et dans tout ce qu'il mange
Retrouve l'ambroisie et le nectar vermeil.

Il joue avec le vent, cause avec le nuage
Et s'enivre en chantant du chemin de la croix;

Et l'Esprit qui le suit dans son pèlerinage
Pleure de le voir gai comme un oiseau des bois.

Tous ceux qu'il veut aimer l'observent avec crainte,
Ou bien, s'enhardissant de sa tranquillité,
Cherchent à qui saura lui tirer une plainte,
Et font sur lui l'essai de leur férocité.

Dans le pain et le vin destinés à sa bouche
Ils mêlent de la cendre avec d'impurs crachats;
Avec hypocrisie ils jettent ce qu'il touche,
Et s'accusent d'avoir mis leurs pieds dans ses pas.

Sa femme va criant sur les places publiques:
« Puisqu'il me trouve assez belle pour m'adorer,
Je ferai le métier des idoles antiques,
Et comme elles je veux me faire redorer;

« Et je me soûlerai de nard, d'encens, de myrrhe,
De génuflexions, de viandes et de vins,
Pour savoir si je puis dans un cœur qui m'admire
Usurper en riant les hommages divins!

« Et, quand je m'ennuîrai de ces farces impies,
Je poserai sur lui ma frêle et forte main;
Et mes ongles, pareils aux ongles des harpies,
Sauront jusqu'à son cœur se frayer un chemin.

« Comme un tout jeune oiseau qui tremble et qui palpite,
J'arracherai ce cœur tout rouge de son sein,
Et, pour rassasier ma bête favorite,
Je le lui jetterai par terre avec dédain! »

Vers le Ciel, où son œil voit un trône splendide,
Le Poète serein lève ses bras pieux,

Et les vastes éclairs de son esprit lucide
Lui dérobent l'aspect des peuples furieux:

« Soyez béni, mon Dieu, qui donnez la souffrance
Comme un divin remède à nos impuretés,
Et comme la meilleure et la plus pure essence
Qui prépare les forts aux saintes voluptés!

« Je sais que vous gardez une place au Poète
Dans les rangs bienheureux des saintes Légions,
Et que vous l'invitez à l'éternelle fête
Des Trônes, des Vertus, des Dominations.

« Je sais que la douleur est la noblesse unique
Où ne mordront jamais la terre et les enfers,
Et qu'il faut pour tresser ma couronne mystique
Imposer tous les temps et tous les univers.

« Mais les bijoux perdus de l'antique Palmyre,
Les métaux inconnus, les perles de la mer,
Par votre main montés, ne pourraient pas suffire
A ce beau diadème éblouissant et clair;

« Car il ne sera fait que de pure lumière,
Puisée au foyer saint des rayons primitifs,
Et dont les yeux mortels, dans leur splendeur entière,
Ne sont que des miroirs obscurcis et plaintifs! »

THE BENEDICTION

When by the high decree of powers supreme,
    The Poet came into this world outworn,
She who had borne him, in a ghastly dream,
    Clenched blasphemous hands at God, and cried in scorn:

"O rather had I borne a writhing knot
    Of unclean vipers, than my breast should nurse
This vile derision, of my joy begot
    To be my expiation and my curse!

"Since of all women thou hast made of me
    Unto my husband a disgust and shame;
Since I may not cast this monstrosity,
    Like an old love-epistle, to the flame;

"I will pour out thine overwhelming hate
    On this the accursed weapon of thy spite;
This stunted tree I will so desecrate
    That not one tainted bud shall see the light!"

So foaming with the foam of hate and shame,
    Blind unto God's design inexorable,
With her own hands she fed the purging flame
    To crimes maternal consecrate in hell.

Meanwhile beneath an Angel's care unseen
    The child disowned grows drunken with the sun;
His food and drink, though they be poor and mean,
    With streams of nectar and ambrosia run.

Speaking to clouds and playing with the wind,
    With joy he sings the sad Way of the Rood;

His shadowing pilgrim spirit weeps behind
    To see him gay as birds are in the wood.

Those he would love looked sideways and with fear,
    Or, taking courage from his aspect mild,
Sought who should first bring to his eye the tear,
    And spent their anger on the dreaming child.

With all the bread and wine the Poet must eat
    They mingled earth and ash and excrement,
All things he touched were spurned beneath their feet;
    They mourned if they must tread the road he went.

His wife ran crying in the public square:
    "Since he has found me worthy to adore,
Shall I not be as antique idols were,
    With gold and with bright colours painted o'er?

"I will be drunk with nard and frankincense.
    With myrrh, and knees bowed down, and flesh and wine.
Can I not, smiling, in his love-sick sense,
    Usurp the homage due to beings divine?

"I will lay on him my fierce, fragile hand
    When I am weary of the impious play;
For well these harpy talons understand
    To furrow to his heart their crimson way.

"I'll tear the red thing beating from his breast,
    To cast it with disdain upon the ground,
Like a young bird torn trembling from the nest –
    His heart shall go to gorge my favourite hound."

To the far heaven, where gleams a splendid throne,
    The Poet uplifts his arms in calm delight,

And the vast beams from his pure spirit flown,
    Wrap all the furious peoples from his sight:

"Thou, O my God, be blest who givest pain,
    The balm divine for each imperfect heart,
The strong pure essence cleansing every stain
    Of sin that keeps us from thy joys apart.

"Among the numbers of thy legions blest,
    I know a place awaits the poet there;
Him thou hast bid attend the eternal feast
    That Thrones and Virtues and Dominions share.

"I know the one thing noble is a grief
    Withstanding earth's and hell's destructive tooth,
And I, through all my dolorous life and brief,
    To gain the mystic crown, must cry the truth.

"The jewels lost in Palmyra of old,
    Metals unknown, pearls of the outer sea,
Are far too dim to set within the gold
    Of the bright crown that Time prepares for me.

"For it is wrought of pure unmingled light,
    Dipped in the white flame whence all flame is born –
The flame that makes all eyes, though diamond-bright,
    Seem obscure mirrors, darkened and forlorn."

BOHÉMIANS EN VOYAGE

La tribu prophétique aux prunelles ardentes
Hier s'est mise en route, emportant ses petits
Sur son dos, ou livrant à leurs fiers appétits
Le trésor toujours prêt des mamelles pendantes.

Les hommes vont à pied sous leurs armes luisantes
Le long des chariots où les leurs sont blottis,
Promenant sur le ciel des yeux appesantis
Par le morne regret des chimères absentes.

Du fond de son réduit sablonneux, le grillon,
Les regardant passer, redouble sa chanson;
Cybèle, qui les aime, augmente ses verdures,

Fait couler le rocher et fleurir le désert
Devant ces voyageurs, pour lesquels est ouvert
L'empire familier des ténèbres futures.

GYPSIES TRAVELLING

The tribe prophetic with the eyes of fire
Went forth last night; their little ones at rest
Each on his mother's back, with his desire
Set on the ready treasure of her breast.

Laden with shining arms the men-folk tread
By the long wagons where their goods lie hidden;
They watch the heaven with eyes grown wearied
Of hopeless dreams that come to them unbidden.

The grasshopper, from out his sandy screen,
Watching them pass redoubles his shrill song;
Dian, who loves them, makes the grass more green,

And makes the rock run water for this throng
Of ever-wandering ones whose calm eyes see
Familiar realms of darkness yet to be.

FRANCISCÆ MEÆ LAUDES

Novis te cantabo chordis,
O novelletum quod ludia
In solitudine cordis.

Esto sertis implicata,
O fœmina delicata
Per quam solvuntur peccata

Sicut beneficum Lethe,
Hauriam oscula de te,
Quæ imbuta es magnete.

Quum vitiorum tempestas
Turbabat omnes semitas,
Apparuisti, Deitas,

Velut stella salutaris
In naufragiis amaris....
Suspendam cor tuis aris!

Piscina plena virtutis,
Fons æternæ juventutis,
Labris vocem redde mutis!

Quod erat spurcum, cremasti;
Quod rudius, exæquasti;
Quod debile, confirmasti!

In fame mea taberna,
In nocte mea lucerna,
Recte me semper guberna.

Adde nunc vires viribus,
Dulce balneum suavibus,
Unguentatum odoribus!

Meos circa I umbos mica,
O castitatis lorica,
Aqua tincta seraphica;

Patera gemmis corusca,
Panis salsus, mollis esca,
Divinum vinum, Francisca!

FRANCISCÆ MEÆ LAUDES[1]

I shall sing new chords, O hind,
As you gambol unconfined
Through my solitary mind.

Rest, adorned with wreaths of flowers,
Comely woman whose vast powers
Wash away these sins of ours

As from Lethe's stream I shall
Drink your kisses, one and all,
Magnet-like and magical.

When our vices stormily
Swept down every path with glee,
You approved, O Deity!

Like the bright star of salvation
Amid shipwreck's desolation –
Take my heart in rapt oblation.

Source of every good and store
Of eternal youth, restore
Song to my mute lips once more.

What was foul you calcinated
What was rough you levigated,
What was weak you stimulated.

In my hunger, you the inn,
In my dark, the lamp; and in
Your pale hands, an end to sin.

---

[1] The poem was not translated originally. This translation is by Jacques Le Clercq.

Add your strength to mine, new-sent,
Sweet bath ever redolent
Of the suaver perfumes blent.

From my loins, gleam radiantly
O cuirass of chastity
Steep in balm seraphically.

Cup with precious gems ashine,
Savory bread, celestial wine,
Blessed food, Francesca mine!

"AVEC SES VETEMENTS ONDOYANTS ET NACRÉS"

Avec ses vêtements ondoyants et nacrés,
Même quand elle marche on croirait qu'elle danse,
Comme ces longs serpents que les jongleurs sacrés
Au bout de leurs bâtons agitent en cadence.

Comme le sable morne et l'azur des déserts,
Insensibles tous deux à l'humaine souffrance
Comme les longs réseaux de la houle des mers
Elle se développe avec indifférence.

Ses yeux polis sont faits de minéraux charmants,
Et dans cette nature étrange et symbolique
Où l'ange inviolé se mêle au sphinx antique,

Où tout n'est qu'or, acier, lumière et diamants,
Resplendit à jamais, comme un astre inutile,
La froide majesté de la femme stérile.

ROBED IN A SILKEN ROBE

Robed in a silken robe that shines and shakes,
    She seems to dance whene'er she treads the sod,
Like the long serpent that a fakir makes
    Dance to the waving cadence of a rod.

As the sad sand upon the desert's verge,
    Insensible to mortal grief and strife;
As the long weeds that float among the surge,
    She folds indifference round her budding life.

Her eyes are carved of minerals pure and cold,
And in her strange symbolic nature where
An angel mingles with the sphinx of old,

Where all is gold and steel and light and air,
For ever, like a vain star, unafraid
Shines the cold hauteur of the sterile maid.

PAYSAGE

Je veux, pour composer chastement mes églogues,
Coucher auprès du ciel, comme les astrologues,
Et, voisin des clochers écouter en rêvant
Leurs hymnes solennels emportés par le vent.
Les deux mains au menton, du haut de ma mansarde,
Je verrai l'atelier qui chante et qui bavarde;
Les tuyaux, les clochers, ces mâts de la cité,
Et les grands ciels qui font rêver d'éternité.

Il est doux, à travers les brumes, de voir naître
L'étoile dans l'azur, la lampe à la fenêtre
Les fleuves de charbon monter au firmament
Et la lune verser son pâle enchantement.
Je verrai les printemps, les étés, les automnes;
Et quand viendra l'hiver aux neiges monotones,
Je fermerai partout portières et volets
Pour bâtir dans la nuit mes féeriques palais.
Alors je rêverai des horizons bleuâtres,
Des jardins, des jets d'eau pleurant dans les albâtres,
Des baisers, des oiseaux chantant soir et matin,
Et tout ce que l'Idylle a de plus enfantin.
L'Emeute, tempêtant vainement à ma vitre,
Ne fera pas lever mon front de mon pupitre;
Car je serai plongé dans cette volupté
D'évoquer le Printemps avec ma volonté,
De tirer un soleil de mon cœur, et de faire
De mes pensers brûlants une tiède atmosphère.

A LANDSCAPE

I would, when I compose my solemn verse,
Sleep near the heaven as do astrologers,
Near the high bells, and with a dreaming mind
Hear their calm hymns blown to me on the wind.

Out of my tower, with chin upon my hands,
I'll watch the singing, babbling human bands;
And see clock-towers like spars against the sky,
And heavens that bring thoughts of eternity;

And softly, through the mist, will watch the birth
Of stars in heaven and lamplight on the earth;
The threads of smoke that rise above the town;
The moon that pours her pale enchantment down.

Seasons will pass till Autumn fades the rose;
And when comes Winter with his weary snows,
I'll shut the doors and window-casements tight,
And build my faery palace in the night.

Then I will dream of blue horizons deep;
Of gardens where the marble fountains weep;
Of kisses, and of ever-singing birds –
A sinless Idyll built of innocent words.

And Trouble, knocking at my window-pane
And at my closet door, shall knock in vain;
I will not heed him with his stealthy tread,
Nor from my reverie uplift my head;

For I will plunge deep in the pleasure still
Of summoning the spring-time with my will,

Drawing the sun out of my heart, and there
With burning thoughts making a summer air.

LE VOYAGE

A MAXIME DU CAMP

I

Pour l'enfant, amoureux de cartes et d'estampes,
L'univers est égal à son vaste appétit.
Ah! que le monde est grand à la clarté des lampes!
Aux yeux du souvenir que le monde est petit!

Un matin nous partons, le cerveau plein de flamme,
Le cœur gros de rancune et de désirs amers,
Et nous allons, suivant le rythme de la lame,
Berçant notre infini sur le fini des mers:

Les uns, joyeux de fuir une patrie infâme;
D'autres, l'horreur de leurs berceaux, et quelques-uns,
Astrologues noyés dans les yeux d'une femme,
La Circé tyrannique aux dangereux parfums.

Pour n'être pas changés en bêtes, ils s'enivrent
D'espace et de lumière et de cieux embrasés;
La glace qui les mord, les soleils qui les cuivrent,
Effacent lentement la marque des baisers.

Mais les vrais voyageurs sont ceux-là seuls qui partent
Pour partir; cœurs légers, semblables aux ballons,
De leur fatalité jamais ils ne s'écartent,
Et, sans savoir pourquoi, disent toujours: Allons!

Ceux-là dont les désirs ont la forme des nues,
Et qui rêvent, ainsi qu'un conscrit le canon,

De vastes voluptés, changeantes, inconnues,
Et dont l'esprit humain n'a jamais su le nom!

II

Nous imitons, horreur! la toupie et la boule
Dans leur valse et leurs bonds; même dans nos sommeils
La Curiosité nous tourmente et nous roule,
Comme un Ange cruel qui fouette des soleils.

Singulière fortune où le but se déplace,
Et, n'étant nulle part, peut être n'importe où!
Où l'Homme, dont jamais l'espérance n'est lasse,
Pour trouver le repos court toujours comme un fou!

Notre âme est un trois-mâts cherchant son Icarie;
Une voix retentit sur le pont: « Ouvre l'œil! »
Une voix de la hune, ardente et folle, crie:
« Amour... gloire... bonheur! » Enfer! c'est un écueil!

Chaque îlot signalé par l'homme de vigie
Est un Eldorado promis par le Destin;
L'Imagination qui dresse son orgie
Ne trouve qu'un récit aux clartés du matin.

O le pauvre amoureux des pays chimériques!
Faut-il le mettre aux fers, le jeter à la mer,
Ce matelot ivrogne, inventeur d'Amériques
Dont le mirage rend le gouffre plus amer?

Tel le vieux vagabond, piétinant dans la boue,
Rêve, le nez en l'air, de brillants paradis;
Son œil ensorcelé découvre une Capoue
Partout où la chandelle illumine un taudis.

III

Etonnants voyageurs! quelles nobles histoires
Nous lisons dans vos yeux profonds comme les mers!
Montrez-nous les écrins de vos riches mémoires,
Les bijoux merveilleux, faits d'astres et d'éthers.

Nous voulons voyager sans vapeur et sans voile!
Faites, pour égayer l'ennui de nos prisons,
Passer sur nos esprits, tendus comme une toile,
Vos souvenirs avec leurs cadres d'horizons.

Dites, qu'avez-vous vu?

IV

    « Nous avons vu des astres
Et des flots; nous avons vu des sables aussi;
Et, malgré bien des chocs et d'imprévus désastres,
Nous nous sommes souvent ennuyés, comme ici.

La gloire du soleil sur la mer violette,
La gloire des cités dans le soleil couchant,
Allumaient dans nos cœurs une ardeur inquiète
De plonger dans un ciel au reflet alléchant.

Les plus riches cités, les plus grands paysages,
Jamais ne contenaient l'attrait mystérieux
De ceux que le hasard fait avec les nuages,
Et toujours le désir nous rendait soucieux!

--La jouissance ajoute au désir de la force.
Désir, vieil arbre à qui le plaisir sert d'engrais,
Cependant que grossit et durcit ton écorce,

Tes branches veulent voir le soleil de plus près!

Grandiras-tu toujours, grand arbre plus vivace
Que le cyprès?--Pourtant nous avons, avec soin,
Cueilli quelques croquis pour votre album vorace,
Frères qui trouvez beau tout ce qui vient de loin!

Nous avons salué des idoles à trompe;
Des trônes constellés de joyaux lumineux;
Des palais ouvragés dont la féerique pompe
Serait pour vos banquiers un rêve ruineux;

Des costumes qui sont pour les yeux une ivresse;
Des femmes dont les dents et les ongles sont teints
Et des jongleurs savants que le serpent caresse. »

V

Et puis, et puis encore?

VI

    « O cerveaux enfantins!
Pour ne pas oublier la chose capitale,
Nous avons vu partout, et sans l'avoir cherché,
Du haut jusques en bas de l'échelle fatale,
Le spectacle ennuyeux de l'immortel péché:

La femme, esclave vile, orgueilleuse et stupide,
Sans rire s'adorant et s'aimant sans dégoût:
L'homme, tyran goulu, paillard, dur et cupide,
Esclave de l'esclave et ruisseau dans l'égout;

Le bourreau qui jouit, le martyr qui sanglote;
La fête qu'assaisonne et parfume le sang;
Le poison du pouvoir énervant le despote,
Et le peuple amoureux du fouet abrutissant;

Plusieurs religions semblables à la nôtre,
Toutes escaladant le ciel; la Sainteté,
Comme en un lit de plume un délicat se vautre,
Dans les clous et le crin cherchant la volupté;

L'Humanité bavarde, ivre de son génie,
Et, folle maintenant comme elle était jadis,
Criant à Dieu, dans sa furibonde agonie:
« O mon semblable, ô mon maître, je te maudis! »

Et les moins sots, hardis amants de la Démence,
Fuyant le grand troupeau parqué par le Destin,
Et se réfugiant dans l'opium immense!
--Tel est du globe entier l'éternel bulletin. »

VII

Amer savoir, celui qu'on tire du voyage!
Le monde, monotone et petit, aujourd'hui,
Hier, demain, toujours, nous fait voir notre image;
Une oasis d'horreur dans un désert d'ennui!

Faut-il partir? rester? Si tu peux rester, reste;
Pars, s'il le faut. L'un court, et l'autre se tapit
Pour tromper l'ennemi vigilant et funeste,
Le Temps! Il est, hélas! des coureurs sans répit,

Comme le Juif errant et comme les apôtres,
A qui rien ne suffit, ni wagon ni vaisseau,

Pour fuir ce rétiaire infâme; il en est d'autres
Qui savent le tuer sans quitter leur berceau.

Lorsque enfin il mettra le pied sur notre échine,
Nous pourrons espérer et crier: En avant!
De même qu'autrefois nous partions pour la Chine,
Les yeux fixés an large et les cheveux au vent,

Nous nous embarquerons sur la mer des Ténèbres
Avec le cœur joyeux d'un jeune passager.
Entendez-vous ces voix, charmantes et funèbres,
Qui chantent: « Par ici! vous qui voulez manger

Le Lotus parfumé! c'est ici qu'on vendange
Les fruits miraculeux dont votre cœur a faim;
Venez vous enivrer de la couleur étrange
De cette après-midi qui n'a jamais de fin? »

A l'accent familier nous devinons le spectre;
Nos Pylades là-bas tendent leurs bras vers nous.
« Pour rafraîchir ton cœur nage vers ton Electre! »
Dit celle dont jadis nous baisions les genoux.

VIII

O Mort, vieux capitaine, il est temps! levons l'ancre!
Ce pays nous ennuie, ô Mort! Appareillons!
Si le ciel et la mer sont noirs comme de l'encre,
Nos cœurs que tu connais sont remplis de rayons!

Verse-nous ton poison pour qu'il nous réconforte!
Nous voulons, tant ce feu nous brûle le cerveau,
Plonger au fond du gouffre, Enfer ou Ciel, qu'importe?
Au fond de l'Inconnu pour trouver du *nouveau!*

THE VOYAGE

I

The world is equal to the child's desire
Who plays with pictures by his nursery fire –
How vast the world by lamplight seems! How small
When memory's eyes look back, remembering all! –

One morning we set forth with thoughts aflame,
Or heart o'erladen with desire or shame;
And cradle, to the song of surge and breeze,
Our own infinity on the finite seas.

Some flee the memory of their childhood's home;
And others flee their fatherland; and some,
Star-gazers drowned within a woman's eyes,
Flee from the tyrant Circe's witcheries;

And, lest they still be changed to beasts, take flight
For the embrasured heavens, and space, and light,
Till one by one the stains her kisses made
In biting cold and burning sunlight fade.

But the true voyagers are they who part
From all they love because a wandering heart
Drives them to fly the Fate they cannot fly;
Whose call is ever "On!" – they know not why.

Their thoughts are like the clouds that veil a star;
They dream of change as warriors dream of war;
And strange wild wishes never twice the same:
Desires no mortal man can give a name.

II

We are like whirling tops and rolling balls –
For even when the sleepy night-time falls,
Old Curiosity still thrusts us on,
Like the cruel Angel who goads forth the sun.

The end of fate fades ever through the air,
And, being nowhere, may be anywhere
Where a man runs, hope waking in his breast,
For ever like a madman, seeking rest.

Our souls are wandering ships outwearied;
And one upon the bridge asks: "What's ahead?"
The topman's voice with an exultant sound
Cries: "Love and Glory!" – then we run aground.

Each isle the pilot signals when 'tis late,
Is El Dorado, promised us by fate –
Imagination, spite of her belief,
Finds, in the light of dawn, a barren reef.

Oh the poor seeker after lands that flee!
Shall we not bind and cast into the sea
This drunken sailor whose ecstatic mood
Makes bitterer still the water's weary flood?

Such is an old tramp wandering in the mire,
Dreaming the paradise of his own desire,
Discovering cities of enchanted sleep
Where'er the light shines on a rubbish heap.

III

Strange voyagers, what tales of noble deeds
Deep in your dim sea-weary eyes one reads!
Open the casket where your memories are,
And show each jewel, fashioned from a star;

For I would travel without sail or wind,
And so, to lift the sorrow from my mind,
Let your long memories of sea-days far fled
Pass o'er my spirit like a sail outspread.

What have you seen?

IV

    "We have seen waves and stars,
And lost sea-beaches, and known many wars,
And notwithstanding war and hope and fear,
We were as weary there as we are here.

"The lights that on the violet sea poured down,
The suns that set behind some far-off town,
Lit in our hearts the unquiet wish to fly
Deep in the glimmering distance of the sky;

"The loveliest countries that rich cities bless,
Never contained the strange wild loveliness
By fate and chance shaped from the floating cloud –
And we were always sorrowful and proud!

"Desire from joy gains strength in weightier measure.
Desire, old tree who draw'st thy sap from pleasure,
Though thy bark thickens as the years pass by,

Thine arduous branches rise towards the sky;

"And wilt thou still grow taller, tree more fair
Than the tall cypress?

    – Thus have we, with care,
Gathered some flowers to please your eager mood,
Brothers who dream that distant things are good!

"We have seen many a jewel-glimmering throne;
And bowed to Idols when wild horns were blown
In palaces whose faery pomp and gleam
To your rich men would be a ruinous dream;

"And robes that were a madness to the eyes;
Women whose teeth and nails were stained with dyes;
Wise jugglers round whose neck the serpent winds – "

V

And then, and then what more?

VI

    "O childish minds!

"Forget not that which we found everywhere,
From top to bottom of the fatal stair,
Above, beneath, around us and within,
The weary pageant of immortal sin.

"We have seen woman, stupid slave and proud,
Before her own frail, foolish beauty bowed;

And man, a greedy, cruel, lascivious fool,
Slave of the slave, a ripple in a pool;

"The martyrs groan, the headsman's merry mood;
And banquets seasoned and perfumed with blood;
Poison, that gives the tyrant's power the slip;
And nations amorous of the brutal whip;

"Many religions not unlike our own,
All in full flight for heaven's resplendent throne;
And Sanctity, seeking delight in pain,
Like a sick man of his own sickness vain;

"And mad mortality, drunk with its own power,
As foolish now as in a bygone hour,
Shouting, in presence of the tortured Christ:
'I curse thee, mine own Image sacrificed.'

"And silly monks in love with Lunacy,
Fleeing the troops herded by destiny,
Who seek for peace in opiate slumber furled –
Such is the pageant of the rolling world!"

VII

O bitter knowledge that the wanderers gain!
The world says our own age is little and vain;
For ever, yesterday, to-day, to-morrow,
'Tis horror's oasis in the sands of sorrow.

Must we depart? If you can rest, remain;
Part, if you must. Some fly, some cower in vain,
Hoping that Time, the grim and eager foe,
Will pass them by; and some run to and fro

Like the Apostles or the Wandering Jew;
Go where they will, the Slayer goes there too!
And there are some, and these are of the wise,
Who die as soon as birth has lit their eyes.

But when at length the Slayer treads us low,
We will have hope and cry, "'Tis time to go!"
As when of old we parted for Cathay
With wind-blown hair and eyes upon the bay.

We will embark upon the Shadowy Sea,
Like youthful wanderers for the first time free –
Hear you the lovely and funereal voice
That sings: *O come all ye whose wandering joys*
Are set upon the scented Lotus flower,
For here we sell the fruit's miraculous boon;
Come ye and drink the sweet and sleepy power
Of the enchanted, endless afternoon.

VIII

O Death, old Captain, it is time, put forth!
We have grown weary of the gloomy north;
Though sea and sky are black as ink, lift sail!
Our hearts are full of light and will not fail.

O pour thy sleepy poison in the cup!
The fire within the heart so burns us up
That we would wander Hell and Heaven through,
Deep in the Unknown seeking something *new*!

LITTLE POEMS IN PROSE

L'ÉTRANGER

– Qui aimes-tu le mieux, homme énigmatique, dis? ton père, ta mère, ta soeur ou ton frère?

– Je n'ai ni père, ni mère, ni soeur, ni frère.

– Tes amis?

– Vous vous servez là d'une parole dont le sens m'est resté jusqu'à ce jour inconnu.

– Ta patrie?

– J'ignore sous quelle latitude elle est située.

– La beauté?

– Je l'aimerais volontiers, déesse et immortelle.

– L'or?

– Je le hais comme vous haïssez Dieu.

– Eh! qu'aimes-tu donc, extraordinaire étranger?

– J'aime les nuages... les nuages qui passent... là-bas... là-bas... les merveilleux nuages!

THE STRANGER

Tell me, enigmatic man, whom do you love best? Your father, your mother, your sister, or your brother?

"I have neither father, nor mother, nor sister, nor brother."

Your friends, then?

"You use a word that until now has had no meaning for me."

Your country?

"I am ignorant of the latitude in which it is situated."

Then Beauty?

"Her I would love willingly, goddess and immortal."

Gold?

"I hate it as you hate your God."

What, then, extraordinary stranger, do you love?

"I love the clouds – the clouds that pass – yonder – the marvellous clouds."

CHACUN SA CHIMÈRE

Sous un grand ciel gris, dans une grande plaine poudreuse, sans chemins, sans gazon, sans un chardon, sans une ortie, je rencontrai plusieurs hommes qui marchaient courbés.

Chacun d'eux portait sur son dos une énorme Chimère, aussi lourde qu'un sac de farine ou de charbon, ou le fourniment d'un fantassin romain.

Mais la monstrueuse bête n'était pas un poids inerte ; au contraire, elle enveloppait et opprimait l'homme de ses muscles élastiques et puissants ; elle s'agrafait avec ses deux vastes griffes à la poitrine de sa monture ; et sa tête fabuleuse surmontait le front de l'homme, comme un de ces casques horribles par lesquels les anciens guerriers espéraient ajouter à la terreur de l'ennemi.

Je questionnai l'un de ces hommes, et je lui demandai où ils allaient ainsi. Il me répondit qu'il n'en savait rien, ni lui, ni les autres ; mais qu'évidemment ils allaient quelque part, puisqu'ils étaient poussés par un invincible besoin de marcher.

Chose curieuse à noter : aucun de ces voyageur n'avait l'air irrité contre la bête féroce suspendue à son cou et collée à son dos ; on eût dit qu'il la considérait comme faisant partie de lui-même. Tous ces visages fatigués et sérieux ne témoignaient d'aucun désespoir ; sous la coupole spleenétique du ciel, les pieds plongés dans la poussière d'un sol aussi désolé que ce ciel, ils cheminaient avec la physionomie résignée de ceux qui sont condamnés à espérer toujours.

Et le cortège passa à côté de moi et s'enfonça dans l'atmosphère de l'horizon, à l'endroit où la surface arrondie de la planète se dérobe à la curiosité du regard humain.

Et pendant quelques instants je m'obstinai à vouloir comprendre ce mystère ; mais bientôt l'irrésistible Indifférence s'abattit sur moi, et j'en fus plus lourdement accablé qu'ils ne l'étaient eux-mêmes par leurs écrasantes Chimères.

EVERY MAN HIS CHIMÆRA

Beneath a broad grey sky, upon a vast and dusty plain devoid of grass, and where not even a nettle or a thistle was to be seen, I met several men who walked bowed down to the ground.

Each one carried upon his back an enormous Chimæra as heavy as a sack of flour or coal, or as the equipment of a Roman foot-soldier.

But the monstrous beast was not a dead weight, rather she enveloped and oppressed the men with her powerful and elastic muscles, and clawed with her two vast talons at the breast of her mount. Her fabulous head reposed upon the brow of the man like one of those horrible casques by which ancient warriors hoped to add to the terrors of the enemy.

I questioned one of the men, asking him why they went so. He replied that he knew nothing, neither he nor the others, but that evidently they went somewhere, since they were urged on by an unconquerable desire to walk.

Very curiously, none of the wayfarers seemed to be irritated by the ferocious beast hanging at his neck and cleaving to his back: one had said that he considered it as a part of himself. These grave and weary faces bore witness to no despair. Beneath the splenetic cupola of the heavens, their feet trudging through the dust of an earth as desolate as the sky, they journeyed onwards with the resigned faces of men condemned to hope for ever. So the train passed me and faded into the atmosphere of the horizon at the place where the planet unveils herself to the curiosity of the human eye.

During several moments I obstinately endeavoured to comprehend this mystery; but irresistible Indifference soon threw herself upon me, nor was I more heavily dejected thereby than they by their crushing Chimæras.

LE FOU ET LA VÉNUS

Quelle admirable journée! Le vaste parc se pâme sous l'oeil brûlant du soleil, comme la jeunesse sous la domination de l'Amour.

L'extase universelle des choses ne s'exprime par aucun bruit; les eaux elles-mêmes sont comme endormies. Bien différente des fêtes humaines, c'est ici une orgie silencieuse.

On dirait qu'une lumière toujours croissante fait de plus en plus étinceler les objets; que les fleurs excitées brûlent du désir de rivaliser avec l'azur du ciel par l'énergie de leurs couleurs, et que la chaleur, rendant visibles les parfums, les fait monter vers l'astre comme des fumées.

Cependant, dans cette jouissance universelle, j'ai aperçu un être affligé.

Aux pieds d'une colossale Vénus, un de ces fous artificiels, un de ces bouffons volontaires chargés de faire rire les rois quand le Remords ou l'Ennui les obsède, affublé d'un costume éclatant et ridicule, coiffé de cornes et de sonnettes, tout ramassé contre le piédestal, lève des yeux pleins de larmes vers l'immortelle Déesse.

Et ses yeux disent: "– Je suis le dernier et le plus solitaire des humains, privé d'amour et d'amitié, et bien inférieur en cela au plus imparfait des animaux. Cependant je suis fait, moi aussi, pour comprendre et sentir l'immortelle Beauté! Ah! Déesse! ayez pitié de ma tristesse et de mon délire!"

Mais l'implacable Vénus regarde au loin je ne sais quoi avec ses yeux de marbre.

VENUS AND THE FOOL

How admirable the day! The vast park swoons beneath the burning eye of the sun, as youth beneath the lordship of love.

There is no rumour of the universal ecstasy of all things. The waters themselves are as though drifting into sleep. Very different from the festivals of humanity, here is a silent revel.

It seems as though an ever-waning light makes all objects glimmer more and more, as though the excited flowers burn with a desire to rival the blue of the sky by the vividness of their colours; as though the heat, making perfumes visible, drives them in vapour towards their star.

Yet, in the midst of this universal joy, I have perceived one afflicted thing.

At the feet of a colossal Venus, one of those motley fools, those willing clowns whose business it is to bring laughter upon kings when weariness or remorse possesses them, lies wrapped in his gaudy and ridiculous garments, coined with his cap and bells, huddled against the pedestal, and raises towards the goddess his eyes filled with tears.

And his eyes say: "I am the last and most alone of all mortals, inferior to the meanest of animals in that I am denied either love or friendship. Yet I am made, even I, for the understanding and enjoyment of immortal Beauty. O Goddess, have pity upon my sadness and my frenzy."

The implacable Venus gazed into I know not what distances with her marble eyes.

ENIVREZ-VOUS

Il faut être toujours ivre. Tout est là: c'est l'unique question. Pour ne pas sentir l'horrible fardeau du Temps qui brise vos épaules et vous penche vers la terre, il faut vous enivrer sans trêve.

Mais de quoi? De vin, de poésie ou de vertu, à votre guise. Mais enivrez-vous.

Et si quelquefois, sur les marches d'un palais, sur l'herbe verte d'un fossé, dans la solitude morne de votre chambre, vous vous réveillez, l'ivresse déjà diminuée ou disparue, demandez au vent, à la vague, à l'étoile, à l'oiseau, à l'horloge, à tout ce qui fuit, à tout ce qui gémit, à tout ce qui roule, à tout ce qui chante, à tout ce qui parle, demandez quelle heure il est; et le vent, la vague, l'étoile, l'oiseau, l'horloge, vous répondront: "Il est l'heure de s'enivrer! Pour n'être pas les esclaves martyrisés du Temps, enivrez-vous; enivrez-vous sans cesse! De vin, de poésie ou de vertu, à votre guise."

INTOXICATION

One must be for ever drunken: that is the sole question of importance. If you would not feel the horrible burden of Time that bruises your shoulders and bends you to the earth, you must be drunken without cease. But how? With wine, with poetry, with virtue, with what you please. But be drunken. And if sometimes, on the steps of a palace, on the green grass by a moat, or in the dull loneliness of your chamber, you should waken up, your intoxication already lessened or gone, ask of the wind, of the wave, of the star, of the bird, of the timepiece; ask of all that flees, all that sighs, all that revolves, all that sings, all that speaks, ask of these the hour; and wind and wave and star and bird and timepiece will answer you: "It is the hour to be drunken! Lest you be the martyred slaves of Time, intoxicate yourselves, be drunken without cease! With wine, with poetry, with virtue, or with what you will."

LES BIENFAITS DE LA LUNE

La Lune, qui est le caprice même, regarda par la fenêtre pendant que tu dormais dans ton berceau, et se dit: "Cette enfant me plaît."

Et elle descendit moelleusement son escalier de nuages et passa sans bruit à travers les vitres. Puis elle s'étendit sur toi avec la tendresse souple d'une mère, et elle déposa ses couleurs sur ta face. Tes prunelles en sont restées vertes, et tes joues extraordinairement pâles. C'est en contemplant cette visiteuse que tes yeux se sont si bizarrement agrandis; et elle t'a si tendrement serrée à la gorge que tu en as gardé pour toujours l'envie de pleurer.

Cependant, dans l'expansion de sa joie, la Lune remplissait toute la chambre comme une atmosphère phosphorique, comme un poison lumineux; et toute cette lumière vivante pensait et disait: "Tu subiras éternellement l'influence de mon baiser. Tu seras belle à ma manière. Tu aimeras ce que j'aime et ce qui m'aime: l'eau, les nuages, le silence et la nuit; la mer immense et verte; l'eau informe et multiforme; le lieu où tu ne seras pas; l'amant que tu ne connaîtras pas; les fleurs monstrueuses; les parfums qui font délirer; les chats qui se pâment sur les pianos, et qui gémissent comme les femmes, d'une voix rauque et douce!

"Et tu serais aimée de mes amants, courtisée par mes courtisans. Tu seras la reine des hommes aux yeux verts dont j'ai serré aussi la gorge dans mes caresses nocturnes; de ceux-là qui aiment la mer, la mer immense, tumultueuse et verte, l'eau informe et multiforme, le lieu où ils ne sont pas, la femme qu'ils ne connaissent pas, les fleurs sinistres qui ressemblent aux encensoirs d'une religion inconnue, les parfums qui troublent la volonté, et les animaux sauvages et voluptueux qui sont les emblèmes de leur folie."

Et c'est pour cela, maudite chère enfant gâtée, que je suis maintenant couché à tes pieds, cherchant dans toute ta personne le reflet de la redoutable Divinité, de la fatidique marraine, de la nourrice empoisonneuse de tous les lunatiques.

THE GIFTS OF THE MOON

The Moon, who is caprice itself, looked in at the window as you slept in your cradle, and said to herself: "I am well pleased with this child."

And she softly descended her stairway of clouds and passed through the window-pane without noise. She bent over you with the supple tenderness of a mother and laid her colours upon your face. Therefrom your eyes have remained green and your cheeks extraordinarily pale. From contemplation of your visitor your eyes are so strangely wide; and she so tenderly wounded you upon the breast that you have ever kept a certain readiness to tears.

In the amplitude of her joy, the Moon filled all your chamber as with a phosphorescent air, a luminous poison; and all this living radiance thought and said: "You shall be for ever under the influence of my kiss. You shall love all that loves me and that I love: clouds, and silence, and night; the vast green sea; the unformed and multitudinous waters; the place where you are not; the lover you will never know; monstrous flowers, and perfumes that bring madness; cats that stretch themselves swooning upon the piano and lament with the sweet, hoarse voices of women.

"And you shall be loved of my lovers, courted of my courtesans. You shall be the Queen of men with green eyes, whose breasts also I have wounded in my nocturnal caress: men that love the sea, the immense green ungovernable sea; the unformed and multitudinous waters; the place where they are not; the woman they will never know; sinister flowers that seem to bear the incense of some unknown religion; perfumes that trouble the will; and all savage and voluptuous animals, images of their own folly."

And that is why I am couched at your feet, O spoiled child, beloved and accursed, seeking in all your being the reflection of that august divinity, that prophetic godmother, that poisonous nurse of all *lunatics*.

L'INVITATION AU VOYAGE

Il est un pays superbe, un pays de Cocagne, dit-on, que je rêve de visiter avec une vieille amie. Pays singulier, noyé dans les brumes de notre Nord, et qu'on pourrait appeler l'Orient de l'Occident, la Chine de l'Europe, tant la chaude et capricieuse fantaisie s'y est donné carrière, tant elle l'a patiemment et opiniâtrement illustré de ses savantes et délicates végétations.

Un vrai pays de Cocagne, où tout est beau, riche, tranquille, honnête; où le luxe a plaisir à se mirer dans l'ordre; où la vie est grasse et douce à respirer; d'où le désordre, la turbulence et l'imprévu sont exclus; où le bonheur est marié au silence; où la cuisine elle-même est poétique, grasse et excitante à la fois; où tout vous ressemble, mon cher ange.

Tu connais cette maladie fiévreuse qui s'empare de nous dans les froides misères, cette nostalgie du pays qu'on ignore, cette angoisse de la curiosité? Il est une contrée qui te ressemble, où tout est beau, riche, tranquille et honnête, où la fantaisie a bâti et décoré une Chine occidentale, où la vie est douce à respirer, où le bonheur est marié au silence. C'est là qu'il faut aller vivre, c'est là qu'il faut aller mourir!

Oui, c'est là qu'il faut aller respirer, rêver et allonger les heures par l'infini des sensations. Un musicien a écrit l'invitation à la valse; quel est celui qui composera l'invitation au voyage, qu'on puisse offrir à la femme aimée, à la soeur d'élection?

Oui, c'est dans cette atmosphère qu'il ferait bon vivre, – là-bas, où les heures plus lentes contiennent plus de pensées, où les horloges sonnent le bonheur avec une plus profonde et plus significative solennité.

Sur des panneaux luisants, ou sur des cuirs dorés et d'une richesse sombre, vivent discrètement des peintures béates, calmes et profondes, comme les âmes des artistes qui les créèrent. Les soleils couchants, qui colorent si richement la salle à manger ou le salon, sont tamisés par de belles étoffes ou par ces hautes fenêtres ouvragées que le plomb divise en nombreux compartiments. Les meubles sont vastes, curieux, bizarres, armés de serrures et de secrets comme des âmes raffinées. Les miroirs, les métaux, les étoiles, l'orfèvrerie et la faïence y jouent pour les yeux une symphonie muette et mystérieuse; et de toutes choses, de tous les coins, des fissures des tiroirs et des plis des étoffes s'échappe un parfum singulier, un revenez-y de Sumatra, qui est comme l'âme de l'appartement.

Un vrai pays de Cocagne, te dis-je, où tout est riche, propre et luisant, comme une belle conscience, comme une magnifique batterie de cuisine, comme une splendide orfèvrerie, comme une bijouterie bariolée! Les trésors du monde y affluent, comme dans la maison d'un homme laborieux et qui a bien mérité du monde entier. Pays singulier, supérieur aux autres, comme l'Art l'est à la Nature, où celle-ci est réformée par le rêve, où elle est corrigée, embellie, refondue.

Qu'ils cherchent, qu'ils cherchent encore, qu'ils reculent sans cesse les limites de leur bonheur, ces alchimistes de l'horticulture! Qu'ils proposent des prix de soixante et de cent mille florins pour qui résoudra leurs ambitieux problèmes! Moi, j'ai trouvé ma tulipe noire et mon dahlia bleu!

Fleur incomparable, tulipe retrouvée, allégorique dahlia, c'est là, n'est-ce pas, dans ce beau pays si calme et si rêveur, qu'il faudrait aller vivre et fleurir? Ne serais-tu pas encadrée dans ton analogie, et ne pourrais-tu pas te mirer, pour parler comme les mystiques, dans ta propre correspondance?

Des rêves! toujours des rêves! et plus l'âme est ambitieuse et délicate, plus les rêves l'éloignent du possible. Chaque homme porte en lui sa dose d'opium naturel, incessamment sécrétée et renouvelée, et, de la naissance à la mort, combien comptons-nous d'heures remplies par la jouissance positive, par l'action réussie et décidée? Vivrons-nous jamais, passerons-nous jamais dans ce tableau qu'a peint mon esprit, ce tableau qui te ressemble?

Ces trésors, ces meubles, ce luxe, cet ordre, ces parfums, ces fleurs miraculeuses, c'est toi. C'est encore toi, ces grands fleuves et ces canaux tranquilles. Ces énormes navires qu'ils charrient, tout chargés de richesses et d'où montent les chants monotones de la manoeuvre, ce sont mes pensées qui dorment ou qui roulent sur ton sein. Tu les conduis doucement vers la mer qui est l'Infini, tout en réfléchissant les profondeurs du ciel dans la limpidité de ta belle âme; – et quand, fatigués par la houle et gorgés des produits de l'Orient, ils rentrent au port natal, ce sont encore mes pensées enrichies qui reviennent de l'Infini vers toi.

THE INVITATION TO THE VOYAGE

It is a superb land, a country of Cockaigne, as they say, that I dream of visiting with an old friend. A strange land, drowned in our northern fogs, that one might call the East of the West, the China of Europe; a land patiently and luxuriously decorated with the wise, delicate vegetations of a warm and capricious phantasy.

A true land of Cockaigne, where all is beautiful, rich, tranquil, and honest; where luxury is pleased to mirror itself in order; where life is opulent, and sweet to breathe; from whence disorder, turbulence, and the unforeseen are excluded; where happiness is married to silence; where even the food is poetic, rich and exciting at the same time; where all things, my beloved, are like you.

Do you know that feverish malady that seizes hold of us in our cold miseries; that nostalgia of a land unknown; that anguish of curiosity? It is a land which resembles you, where all is beautiful, rich, tranquil and honest, where phantasy has built and decorated an occidental China, where life is sweet to breathe, and happiness married to silence. It is there that one would live; there that one would die.

Yes, it is there that one must go to breathe, to dream, and to lengthen one's hours by an infinity of sensations. A musician has written the "Invitation to the Waltz"; where is he who will write the "Invitation to the Voyage," that one may offer it to his beloved, to the sister of his election?

Yes, it is in this atmosphere that it would be good to live, – yonder, where slower hours contain more thoughts, where the clocks strike the hours of happiness with a more profound and significant solemnity.

Upon the shining panels, or upon skins gilded with a sombre opulence, beatified paintings have a discreet life, as calm and profound as the souls of the artists who created them.

The setting suns that colour the rooms and salons with so rich a light, shine through veils of rich tapestry, or through high leaden-worked windows of many compartments. The furniture is massive, curious, and bizarre, armed with locks and secrets, like profound and refined souls. The mirrors, the metals, the ail ver work and the china, play a mute and mysterious symphony for the eyes; and from all things, from the corners, from the chinks in the drawers, from the folds of drapery, a singular perfume escapes, a Sumatran *revenez-y*, which is like the soul of the apartment.

A true country of Cockaigne, I have said; where all is rich, correct and shining, like a beautiful conscience, or a splendid set of silver, or a medley of jewels. The treasures of the world flow there, as in the house of a laborious man who has well merited the entire world. A singular land, as superior to others as Art is superior to Nature; where Nature is made over again by dream; where she is corrected, embellished, refashioned.

Let them seek and seek again, let them extend the limits of their happiness for ever, these alchemists who work with flowers! Let them offer a prize of sixty or a hundred thousand florins to whosoever can solve their ambitious problems! As for me, I have found my *black tulip* and my *blue dahlia*!

Incomparable flower, tulip found at last, symboli-cal dahlia, it is there, is it not, in this so calm and dreamy land that you live and blossom? Will you not there be framed in your proper analogy, and will you not be mirrored, to speak like the mystics, in your own *correspondence*?

Dreams! – always dreams! and the more ambitious and delicate the soul, the farther from possibility is the dream. Every man carries within him his dose of natural opium, incessantly secreted and renewed, and, from birth to death, how many hours can we count that have been filled with positive joy, with successful and decided action? Shall we ever live in and become a part of the picture my spirit has painted, the picture that resembles you?

These treasures, furnishings, luxury, order, perfumes and

miraculous flowers, are you. You again are the great rivers and calm canals. The enormous ships drifting beneath their loads of riches, and musical with the sailors' monotonous song, are my thoughts that sleep and stir upon your breast. You take them gently to the sea that is Infinity, reflecting the profundities of the sky in the limpid waters of your lovely soul; – and when, outworn by the surge and gorged with the products of the Orient, the ships come back to the ports of home, they are still my thoughts, grown rich, that have returned to you from Infinity.

LAQUELLE EST LA VRAIE?

J'ai connu une certaine Bénédicta, qui remplissait l'atmosphère d'idéal, et dont les yeux répandaient le désir de la grandeur, de la beauté, de la gloire et de tout ce qui fait croire à l'immortalité.

Mais cette fille miraculeuse était trop belle pour vivre longtemps, aussi est-elle morte quelques jours après que j'eus fait sa connaissance, et c'est moi-même qui l'ai enterrée, un jour que le printemps agitait son encensoir jusque dans les cimetières. C'est moi qui l'ai enterrée, bien close dans une bière d'un bois parfumé et incorruptible comme les coffres de l'Inde.

Et comme mes yeux restaient fichés sur le lieu où était enfoui mon trésor, je vis subitement une petite personne qui ressemblait singulièrement à la défunte, et qui, piétinant sur la terre fraîche avec une violence hystérique et bizarre, disait en éclatant de rire:

"C'est moi, la vraie Bénédicta! C'est moi, une fameuse canaille! Et pour la punition de ta folie et de ton aveuglement, tu m'aimeras telle que je suis!"

Mais moi, furieux, j'ai répondu: "Non! non! non!" Et pour mieux accentuer mon refus, j'ai frappé si violemment la terre du pied que ma jambe s'est enfoncée jusqu'au genou dans la sépulture récente, et que, comme un loup pris au piège, je reste attaché, pour toujours peut-être, à la fosse de l'idéal.

WHAT IS TRUTH?

I once knew a certain Benedicta whose presence ailed the air with the ideal and whose eyes spread abroad the desire of grandeur, of beauty, of glory, and of all that makes man believe in immortality.

But this miraculous maiden was too beautiful for long life, so she died soon after I knew her first, and it was I myself who entombed her, upon a day when spring swung her censer even in the burial-ground. It was I myself who entombed her, fast closed in a coffin of perfumed wood, as uncorruptible as the coffers of India.

And, as my eyes rested upon the spot where my treasure lay hidden, I became suddenly aware of a little being who singularly resembled the dead; and who, stamping the newly-turned earth with a curious and hysterical violence, burst into laughter, and said: "It is I, the true Benedicta! It is I, the notorious drab! As the punishment of your folly and blindness you shall love me as I truly am."

But I, furious, replied: "No!" The better to emphasise my refusal I struck the ground so violently with my foot that my leg was thrust up to the knee in the recent grave, and I, like a wolf in a trap, was caught perhaps for ever in the Grave of the Ideal.

DÉJÀ

Cent fois déjà le soleil avait jailli, radieux ou attristé, de cette cuve immense de la mer dont les bords ne se laissent qu'à peine apercevoir; cent fois il s'était replongé, étincelant ou morose, dans son immense bain du soir. Depuis nombre de jours, nous pouvions contempler l'autre côté du firmament et déchiffrer l'alphabet céleste des antipodes. Et chacun des passagers gémissait et grognait. On eût dit que l'approche de la terre exaspérait leur souffrance.

"Quand donc, disaient-ils, cesserons-nous de dormir un sommeil secoué par la lame, troublé par un vent qui ronfle plus haut que nous? Quand pourrons-nous manger de la viande qui ne soit pas salée comme l'élément infâme qui nous porte? Quand pourrons-nous digérer dans un fauteuil immobile?"

Il y en avait qui pensaient à leur foyer, qui regrettaient leurs femmes infidèles et maussades, et leur progéniture criarde. Tous étaient si affolés par l'image de la terre absente, qu'ils auraient, je crois, mangé de l'herbe avec plus d'enthousiasme que les bêtes.

Enfin un rivage fut signalé; et nous vîmes, en approchant, que c'était une terre magnifique, éblouissante. Il semblait que les musiques de la vie s'en détachaient en un vague murmure, et que de ces côtes, riches en verdures de toute sorte, s'exhalait, jusqu'à plusieurs lieues, une délicieuse odeur de fleurs et de fruits.

Aussitôt chacun fut joyeux, chacun abdiqua sa mauvaise humeur. Toutes les querelles furent oubliées, tous les torts réciproques pardonnés; les duels convenus furent rayés de la mémoire, et les rancunes s'envolèrent comme des fumées.

Moi seul j'étais triste, inconcevablement triste. Semblable à un prêtre à qui on arracherait sa divinité, je ne pouvais, sans une navrante amertume, me détacher de cette mer si monstrueusement séduisante, de cette mer si infiniment variée dans son effrayante simplicité, et qui semble contenir en elle et représenter par ses jeux, ses allures, ses colères et ses sourires, les humeurs, les agonies et les extases de toutes les âmes qui ont vécu, qui vivent et qui vivront!

En disant adieu à cette incomparable beauté, je me sentais abattu jusqu'à la mort; et c'est pourquoi, quand chacun de mes compagnons dit: "Enfin!" je ne pus crier que: "*Déjà!*"

Cependant c'était la terre, la terre avec ses bruits, ses passions, ses commodités, ses fêtes; c'était une terre riche et magnifique, pleine de promesses, qui nous envoyait un mystérieux parfum de rose et de musc, et d'où les musiques de la vie nous arrivaient en un amoureux murmure.

ALREADY!

A hundred times already the sun had leaped, radiant or saddened, from the immense cup of the sea whose rim could scarcely be seen; a hundred times it had again sunk, glittering or morose, into its mighty bath of twilight. For many days we had contemplated the other side of the firmament, and deciphered the celestial alphabet of the antipodes. And each of the passengers sighed and complained. One had said that the approach of land only exasperated their sufferings. "When, then," they said, "shall we cease to sleep a sleep broken by the surge, troubled by a wind that snores louder than we? When shall we be able to eat at an unmoving table?"

There were those who thought of their own firesides, who regretted their sullen, faithless wives, and their noisy progeny. All so doted upon the image of the absent land, that I believe they would have eaten grass with as much enthusiasm as the beasts.

At length a coast was signalled, and on approaching we saw a magnificent and dazzling land. It seemed as though the music of life flowed therefrom in a vague murmur; and the banks, rich with all kinds of growths, breathed, for leagues around, a delicious odour of flowers and fruits.

Each one therefore was joyful; his evil humour left him. Quarrels were forgotten, reciprocal wrongs forgiven, the thought of duels was blotted out of the memory, and rancour fled away like smoke.

I alone was sad, inconceivably sad. Like a priest from whom one has torn his divinity, I could not, without heartbreaking bitterness, leave this so monstrously seductive ocean, this sea so infinitely various in its terrifying simplicity, which seemed to contain in itself and represent by its joys, and attractions, and angers, and smiles, the moods and agonies and ecstasies of all souls that have lived, that live, and that shall yet live.

In saying good-bye to this incomparable beauty I felt as though I had been smitten to death; and that is why when each of my companions said: "At last!" I could only cry "*Already!*"

Here meanwhile was the land, the land with its noises, its passions, its commodities, its festivals: a land rich and magnificent, full of promises, that sent to us a mysterious perfume of rose and musk, and from whence the music of life flowed in an amorous murmuring.

LA CHAMBRE DOUBLE

Une chambre qui ressemble à une rêverie, une chambre véritablement spirituelle, où l'atmosphère stagnante est légèrement teintée de rose et de bleu.

L'âme y prend un bain de paresse, aromatisé par le regret et le désir. — C'est quelque chose de crépusculaire, de bleuâtre et de rosâtre; un rêve de volupté pendant une éclipse.

Les meubles ont des formes allongées, prostrées, alanguies. Les meubles ont l'air de rêver; on les dirait doués d'une vie somnambulique, comme le végétal et le minéral. Les étoffes parlent une langue muette, comme les fleurs, comme les ciels, comme les soleils couchants.

Sur les murs nulle abomination artistique. Relativement au rêve pur, à l'impression non analysée, l'art défini, l'art positif est un blasphème. Ici, tout a la suffisante clarté et la délicieuse obscurité de l'harmonie.

Une senteur infinitésimale du choix le plus exquis, à laquelle se mêle une très-légère humidité, nage dans cette atmosphère, où l'esprit sommeillant est bercé par des sensations de serre chaude.

La mousseline pleut abondamment devant les fenêtres et devant le lit; elle s'épanche en cascades neigeuses. Sur ce lit est couchée l'Idole, la souveraine des rêves. Mais comment est-elle ici? Qui l'a amenée? quel pouvoir magique l'a installée sur ce trône de rêverie et de volupté? Qu'importe? la voilà! je la reconnais.

Voilà bien ces yeux dont la flamme traverse le crépuscule; ces subtiles et terribles mirettes, que je reconnais à leur effrayante malice! Elles attirent, elles subjuguent, elles dévorent le regard de l'imprudent qui les contemple. Je les ai souvent étudiées, ces étoiles noires qui commandent la curiosité et l'admiration.

A quel démon bienveillant dois-je d'être ainsi entouré de mystère, de silence, de paix et de parfums? O béatitude! ce que nous nommons généralement la vie, même dans son expansion la plus heureuse, n'a rien de commun avec cette vie suprême dont j'ai maintenant connaissance et que je savoure minute par minute, seconde par seconde!

Non! il n'est plus de minutes, il n'est plus de secondes! Le temps a disparu; c'est l'Eternité qui règne, une éternité de délices!

Mais un coup terrible, lourd, a retenti à la porte, et, comme dans les rêves infernaux, il m'a semblé que je recevais un coup de pioche dans l'estomac.

Et puis un Spectre est entré. C'est un huissier qui vient me torturer au nom de la loi; une infâme concubine qui vient crier misère et ajouter les trivialités de sa vie aux douleurs de la mienne; ou bien le saute-ruisseau d'un directeur de journal qui réclame la suite du manuscrit.

La chambre paradisiaque, l'idole, la souveraine des rêves, la *Sylphide*, comme disait le grand René, toute cette magie a disparu au coup brutal frappé par le Spectre.

Horreur! je me souviens! je me souviens! Oui! ce taudis, ce séjour de l'éternel ennui, est bien le mien. Voici les meubles sots, poudreux, écornés; la cheminée sans flamme et sans braise, souillée de crachats, les tristes fenêtres où la pluie a tracé des sillons dans la poussière; les manuscrits, raturés ou incomplets; l'almanach où le crayon a marqué les dates sinistres!

Et ce parfum d'un autre monde, dont je m'enivrais avec une sensibilité perfectionnée, hélas! il est remplacé par une fétide odeur de tabac mêlée à je ne sais quelle nauséabonde moisissure. On respire ici maintenant le ranci de la désolation.

Dans ce monde étroit, mais si plein de dégoût, un seul objet connu me sourit: la fiole de laudanum; une vieille et terrible amie; comme toutes les amitiés, hélas! féconde en caresses et en traîtrises.

Oh! oui! le Temps a reparu; le Temps règne en souverain maintenant; et avec le hideux vieillard est revenu tout son démoniaque cortège de Souvenirs, de Regrets, de Spasmes, de Peurs, d'Angoisses de cauchemars, de Colères et de Névroses.

Je vous assure que les secondes maintenant sont fortement et solennellement accentuées, et chacune, en jaillissant de la pendule, dit: " — Je suis la Vie, l'insupportable, l'implacable Vie!"

Il n'y a qu'une Seconde dans la vie humaine qui ait mission d'annoncer une bonne nouvelle, la bonne nouvelle qui cause à chacun une inexplicable peur.

Oui! le Temps règne; il a repris sa brutale dictature. Et il me pousse, comme si j'étais un boeuf, avec son double aiguillon. " — Et hue donc! bourrique! Hue donc, esclave! Vis donc, damné!"

THE DOUBLE CHAMBER

A chamber that is like a reverie; a chamber truly *spiritual*, where the stagnant atmosphere is lightly touched with rose and blue.

There the soul bathes itself in indolence made odorous with regret and desire. There is some sense of the twilight, of things tinged with blue and rose: a dream of delight during an eclipse. The shape of the furniture is elongated, low, languishing; one would think it endowed with the somnambulistic vitality of plants and minerals.

The tapestries speak an inarticulate language, like the flowers, the skies, the dropping suns.

There are no artistic abominations upon the walls. Compared with the pure dream, with an impression unanalysed, definite art, positive art, is a blasphemy. Here all has the sufficing lucidity and the delicious obscurity of music.

An infinitesimal odour of the most exquisite choice, mingled with a floating humidity, swims in this atmosphere where the drowsing spirit is lulled by the sensations one feels in a hothouse.

The abundant muslin flows before the windows and the couch, and spreads out in snowy cascades. Upon the couch lies the Idol, ruler of my dreams. But why is she here? – who has brought her? – what magical power has installed her upon this throne of delight and reverie? What matter – she is there; and I recognise her.

These indeed are the eyes whose flame pierces the twilight; the subtle and terrible mirrors that I recognise by their horrifying malice. They attract, they dominate, they devour the sight of whomsoever is imprudent enough to look at them. I have often studied them; these Black Stars that compel curiosity and admiration.

To what benevolent demon, then, do I owe being thus surrounded with mystery, with silence, with peace, and sweet odours? O beatitude! the thing we name life, even in its most fortunate amplitude, has nothing in common with this supreme life with which I am now acquainted, which I taste minute by minute, second by second.

Not so! Minutes are no more; seconds are no more. Time has vanished, and Eternity reigns – an Eternity of delight.

A heavy and terrible knocking reverberates upon the door, and, as in a hellish dream, it seems to me as though I had received a blow from a mattock.

Then a Spectre enters: it is an usher who comes to torture me in the name of the Law; an infamous concubine who comes to cry misery and to add the trivialities of her life to the sorrow of mine; or it may be the errand-boy of an editor who comes to implore the remainder of a manuscript.

The chamber of paradise, the Idol, the ruler of dreams, the Sylphide, as the great René said; all this magic has vanished at the brutal knocking of the Spectre.

Horror; I remember, I remember! Yes, this kennel, this habitation of eternal weariness, is indeed my own. Here is my senseless furniture, dusty and tattered; the dirty fireplace without a flame or an ember; the sad windows where the raindrops have traced runnels in the dust; the manuscripts, erased or unfinished; the almanac with the sinister days marked off with a pencil!

And this perfume of another world, whereof I intoxicated myself with a so perfected sensitiveness; alas, its place is taken by an odour of stale tobacco smoke, mingled with I know not what nauseating mustiness. Now one breathes here the rankness of desolation.

In this narrow world, narrow and yet full of disgust, a single familiar object smiles at me: the phial of laudanum: old and terrible love; like all loves, alas! fruitful in caresses and treacheries.

Yes, Time has reappeared; Time reigns a monarch now; and with the hideous Ancient has returned all his demoniacal following of Memories, Regrets, Tremors, Fears, Dolours, Nightmares, and twittering nerves.

I assure you that the seconds are strongly and solemnly accentuated now; and each, as it drips from the pendulum, says: "I am Life: intolerable, implacable Life!"

There is not a second in mortal life whose mission it is to bear good news: the good news that brings the inexplicable tear to the eye.

Yes, Time reigns; Time has regained his brutal mastery. And he goads me, as though I were a steer, with his double goad: "Woa, thou fool! Sweat, then, thou slave! Live on, thou damnèd!"

À UNE HEURE DU MATIN

Enfin! seul! On n'entend plus que le roulement de quelques fiacres attardés et éreintés. Pendant quelques heures, nous posséderons le silence, sinon le repos. Enfin! la tyrannie de la face humaine a disparu, et je ne souffrirai plus que par moi-même.

Enfin! il m'est donc permis de me délasser dans un bain de ténèbres! D'abord, un double tour à la serrure. Il me semble que ce tour de clef augmentera ma solitude et fortifiera les barricades qui me séparent actuellement du monde.

Horrible vie! Horrible ville! Récapitulons la journée: avoir vu plusieurs hommes de lettres, dont l'un m'a demandé si l'on pouvait aller en Russie par voie de terre (il prenait sans doute la Russie pour une île); avoir disputé généreusement contre le directeur d'une revue, qui à chaque objection répondait: " — C'est ici le parti des honnêtes gens," ce qui implique que tous les autres journaux sont rédigés par des coquins; avoir salué une vingtaine de personnes, dont quinze me sont inconnues; avoir distribué des poignées de main dans la même proportion, et cela sans avoir pris la précaution d'acheter des gants; être monté pour tuer le temps, pendant une averse, chez une sauteuse qui m'a prié de lui dessiner un costume de *Vénustre*; avoir fait ma cour à un directeur de théâtre, qui m'a dit en me congédiant: " — Vous feriez peut-être bien de vous adresser à Z...; c'est le plus lourd, le plus sot et le plus célèbre de tous mes auteurs, avec lui vous pourriez peut-être aboutir à quelque chose. Voyez-le, et puis nous verrons;" m'être vanté (pourquoi?) de plusieurs vilaines actions que je n'ai jamais commises, et avoir lâchement nié quelques autres méfaits que j'ai accomplis avec joie, délit de fanfaronnade, crime de respect humain; avoir refusé à un ami un service facile, et donné une recommandation écrite à un parfait drôle; ouf! est-ce bien fini?

Mécontent de tous et mécontent de moi, je voudrais bien me racheter et m'enorgueillir un peu dans le silence et la solitude de la nuit. Ames de ceux que j'ai aimés, âmes de ceux que j'ai chantés, fortifiez-moi, soutenez-moi, éloignez de moi le mensonge et les vapeurs corruptrices du monde, et vous, Seigneur mon Dieu! accordez-moi la grâce de produire quelques beaux vers qui me prouvent à moi-même que je ne suis pas le dernier des hommes, que je ne suis pas inférieur à ceux que je méprise!

AT ONE O'CLOCK IN THE MORNING

Alone at last! Nothing is to be heard but the rattle of a few tardy and tired-out cabs. There will be silence now, if not repose, for several hours at least. At last the tyranny of the human face has disappeared – I shall not suffer except alone. At last it is permitted me to refresh myself in a bath of shadows. But first a double turn of the key in the lock. It seems to me that this turn of the key will deepen my solitude and strengthen the barriers which actually separate me from the world.

A horrible life and a horrible city! Let us run over the events of the day. I have seen several literary men; one of them wished to know if he could get to Russia by land (he seemed to have an idea that Russia was an island); I have disputed generously enough with the editor of a review, who to each objection replied: "We take the part of respectable people," which implies that every other paper but his own is edited by a knave; I have saluted some twenty people, fifteen of them unknown to me; and shaken hands with a like number, without having taken the precaution of first buying gloves; I have been driven to kill time, during a shower, with a mountebank, who wanted me to design for her a costume as Venusta; I have made my bow to a theatre manager, who said: "You will do well, perhaps, to interview Z; he is the heaviest, foolishest, and most celebrated of all my authors; with him perhaps you will be able to come to something. See him, and then we'll see," I have boasted (why?) of several villainous deeds I never committed, and indignantly denied certain shameful things I accomplished with joy, certain misdeeds of fanfaronade, crimes of human respect; I have refused an easy favour to a friend and given a written recommendation to a perfect fool. Heavens! it's well ended.

Discontented with myself and with everything and everybody else, I should be glad enough to redeem myself and regain my self-respect in the silence and solitude.

Souls of those whom I have loved, whom I have sung, fortify me; sustain me; drive away the lies and the corrupting vapours of this world; and Thou, Lord my God, accord me so much grace as shall produce some beautiful verse to prove to myself that I am not the last of men, that I am not inferior to those I despise.

LA CONFITEOR DE L'ARTISTE

Que les fins de journées d'automne sont pénétrantes! Ah! pénétrantes jusqu'à la douleur! car il est de certaines sensations délicieuses dont le vague n'exclut pas l'intensité; et il n'est pas de pointe plus acérée que celle de l'Infini.

Grand délice que celui de noyer son regard dans l'immensité du ciel et de la mer! Solitude, silence, incomparable chasteté de l'azur! une petite voile frissonnante à l'horizon, et qui par sa petitesse et son isolement imite mon irrémédiable existence, mélodie monotone de la houle, toutes ces choses pensent par moi, ou je pense par elles (car dans la grandeur de la rêverie, le moi se perd vite!); elles pensent, dis-je, mais musicalement et pittoresquement, sans arguties, sans syllogismes, sans déductions.

Toutefois, ces pensées, qu'elles sortent de moi ou s'élancent des choses, deviennent bientôt trop intenses. L'énergie dans la volupté crée un malaise et une souffrance positive. Mes nerfs trop tendus ne donnent plus que des vibrations criardes et douloureuses.

Et maintenant la profondeur du ciel me consterne, sa limpidité m'exaspère. L'insensibilité de la mer, l'immuabilité du spectacle me révoltent... Ah! faut-il éternellement souffrir, ou fuir éternellement le beau?

Nature, enchanteresse sans pitié, rivale toujours victorieuse, laisse-moi! Cesse de tenter mes désirs et mon orgueil! L'étude du beau est un duel où l'artiste crie de frayeur avant d'être vaincu.

THE CONFITEOR OF THE ARTIST

How penetrating is the end of an autumn day! Ah, yes, penetrating enough to be painful even; for there are certain delicious sensations whose vagueness does not prevent them from being intense; and none more keen than the perception of the Infinite. He has a great delight who drowns his gaze in the immensity of sky and sea. Solitude, silence, the incomparable chastity of the azure – a little sail trembling upon the horizon, by its very littleness and isolation imitating my irremediable existence – the melodious monotone of the surge – all these things thinking through me and I through them (for in the grandeur of the reverie the Ego is swiftly lost); they think, I say, but musically and picturesquely, without quibbles, without syllogisms, without deductions.

These thoughts, as they arise in me or spring forth from external objects, soon become always too intense. The energy working within pleasure creates an uneasiness, a positive suffering. My nerves are too tense to give other than clamouring and dolorous vibrations.

And now the profundity of the sky dismays me! its limpidity exasperates me. The insensibility of the sea, the immutability of the spectacle, revolt me. Ah, must one eternally suffer, for ever be a fugitive from Beauty?

Nature, pitiless enchantress, ever-victorious rival, leave me! Tempt my desires and my pride no more. The contemplation of Beauty is a duel where the artist screams with terror before being vanquished.

LE THYRSE

À Franz Liszt

Qu'est-ce qu'un thyrse? Selon le sens moral et poétique, c'est un emblème sacerdotal dans la main des prêtres ou prêtresses célébrant la divinité dont ils sont les interprètes et les serviteurs. Mais physiquement ce n'est qu'un bâton, un pur bâton, perche à houblon, tuteur de vigne, sec, dur et droit. Autour de ce bâton, dans des méandres capricieux, se jouent et folâtrent des tiges et des fleurs, celles-ci sinueuses et fuyardes, celles-là penchées comme des cloches ou des coupes renversées. Et une gloire étonnante jaillit de cette complexité de lignes et de couleurs, tendres ou éclatantes. Ne dirait-on pas que la ligne courbe et la spirale font leur cour à la ligne droite et dansent autour dans une muette adoration? Ne dirait-on pas que toutes ces corolles délicates, tous ces calices, explosions de senteurs et de couleurs, exécutent un mystique fandango autour du bâton hiératique? Et quel est, cependant, le mortel imprudent qui osera décider si les fleurs et les pampres ont été faits pour le bâton, ou si le bâton n'est que le prétexte pour montrer la beauté des pampres et des fleurs? Le thyrse est la représentation de votre étonnante dualité, maître puissant et vénéré, cher Bacchant de la Beauté mystérieuse et passionnée. Jamais nymphe exaspérée par l'invincible Bacchus ne secoua son thyrse sur les têtes de ses compagnes affolées avec autant d'énergie et de caprice que vous agitez votre génie sur les coeurs de vos frères. — Le bâton, c'est votre volonté, droite, ferme et inébranlable; les fleurs, c'est la promenade de votre fantaisie autour de votre volonté; c'est l'élément féminin exécutant autour du mâle ses prestigieuses pirouettes. Ligne droite et ligne arabesque, intention et expression, roideur de la volonté, sinuosité du verbe, unité du but, variété des moyens, amalgame tout-puissant et indivisible du génie, quel analyste aura le détestable courage de vous diviser et de vous séparer?

Cher Liszt, à travers les brumes, par delà les fleuves, par-dessus les villes où les pianos chantent votre gloire, ou l'imprimerie traduit votre sagesse, en quelque lieu que vous soyez, dans les splendeurs de la ville éternelle ou dans les brumes des pays rêveurs que console Cambrinus, improvisant des chants de délectation ou d'ineffable douleur, ou confiant au papier vos méditations abstruses, chantre de la Volupté et de l'Angoisse éternelles, philosophe, poëte et artiste, je vous salue en l'immortalité!

THE THYRSUS

TO FRANZ LISZT

What is a thyrsus? According to the moral and poetical sense, it is a sacerdotal emblem in the hand of the priests or priestesses celebrating the divinity of whom they are the interpreters and servants. But physically it is no more than a baton, a pure staff, a hop-pole, a vine-prop; dry, straight, and hard. Around this baton, in capricious meanderings, stems and flowers twine and wanton; these, sinuous and fugitive; those, hanging like bells or inverted cups. And an astonishing complexity disengages itself from this complexity of tender or brilliant lines and colours. Would not one suppose that the curved line and the spiral pay their court to the straight line, and twine about it in a mute adoration? Would not one say that all these delicate corollæ, all these calices, explosions of odours and colours, execute a mystical dance around the hieratic staff? And what imprudent mortal will dare to decide whether the flowers and the vine branches have been made for the baton, or whether the baton is not but a pretext to set forth the beauty of the vine branches and the flowers?

The thyrsus is the symbol of your astonishing duality, O powerful and venerated master, dear bacchanal of a mysterious and impassioned Beauty. Never a nymph excited by the mysterious Dionysius shook her thyrsus over the heads of her companions with as much energy as your genius trembles in the hearts of your brothers. The baton is your will: erect, firm, unshakeable; the flowers are the wanderings of your fancy around it: the feminine element encircling the masculine with her illusive dance. Straight line and arabesque – intention and expression – the rigidity of the will and the suppleness of the word – a variety of means united for a single purpose – the all-powerful and indivisible amalgam that is genius – what analyst will have the detestable courage to divide or to separate you?

Dear Liszt, across the fogs, beyond the flowers, in towns where the pianos chant your glory, where the printing-house translates your wisdom; in whatever place you be, in the splendour of the Eternal City or among the fogs of the dreamy towns that Cambrinus consoles; improvising rituals of delight or ineffable pain, or giving to paper your abstruse meditations; singer of eternal pleasure and pain, philosopher, poet, and artist, I offer you the salutation of immortality!

LE GALANT TIREUR

Comme la voiture traversait le bois, il la fit arrêter dans le voisinage d'un tir, disant qu'il lui serait agréable de tirer quelques balles pour tuer le Temps. Tuer ce monstre-là, n'est-ce pas l'occupation la plus ordinaire et la plus légitime de chacun? — Et il offrit galamment la main à sa chère, délicieuse et exécrable femme, à cette mystérieuse femme à laquelle il doit tant de plaisirs, tant de douleurs, et peut-être aussi une grande partie de son génie.

Plusieurs balles frappèrent loin du but proposé; l'une d'elles s'enfonça même dans le plafond; et comme la charmante créature riait follement, se moquant de la maladresse de son époux, celui-ci se tourna brusquement vers elle, et lui dit: "Observez cette poupée, là-bas, à droite, qui porte le nez en l'air et qui a la mine si hautaine. Eh bien! cher ange, Je me figure que c'est vous." Et il ferma les yeux et il lâcha la détente. La poupée fut nettement décapitée.

Alors s'inclinant vers sa chère, sa délicieuse, son exécrable femme, son inévitable et impitoyable Muse, et lui baisant respectueusement la main, il ajouta: "Ah! mon cher ange, combien je vous remercie de mon adresse!"

THE MARKSMAN

As the carriage traversed the wood he bade the driver draw up in the neighbourhood of a shooting gallery, saying that he would like to have a few shots to kill time. Is not the slaying of the monster Time the most ordinary and legitimate occupation of man? – So he gallantly offered his hand to his dear, adorable, and execrable wife; the mysterious woman to whom he owed so many pleasures, so many pains, and perhaps also a great part of his genius.

Several bullets went wide of the proposed mark, one of them flew far into the heavens, and as the charming creature laughed deliriously, mocking the clumsiness of her husband, he turned to her brusquely and said: "Observe that doll yonder, to the right, with its nose in the air, and with so haughty an appearance. Very well, dear angel, *I will imagine to myself that it is you!*"

He closed both eyes and pulled the trigger. The doll was neatly decapitated.

Then, bending towards his dear, adorable, and execrable wife, his inevitable and pitiless muse, he kissed her respectfully upon the hand, and added, "Ah, dear angel, how I thank you for my skill!"

LE TIR ET LE CIMETIÈRE

— *A la vue du cimetière, Estaminet.* " — Singulière enseigne, — se dit notre promeneur, — mais bien faite pour donner soif! A coup sûr, le maître de ce cabaret sait apprécier Horace et les poëtes élèves d'Epicure.

Peut-être même connaît-il le raffinement profond des anciens Egyptiens, pour qui il n'y avait pas de bon festin sans squelette, ou sans un emblème quelconque de la brièveté de la vie."

Et il entra, but un verre de bière en face des tombes, et fuma lentement un cigare. Puis la fantaisie le prit de descendre dans ce cimetière, dont l'herbe était si haute et si invitante, et où régnait un si riche soleil.

En effet, la lumière et la chaleur y faisaient rage, et l'on eût dit que le soleil ivre se vautrait tout de son long sur un tapis de fleurs magnifiques engraissées par la destruction. Un immense bruissement de vie remplissait l'air — la vie des infiniment petits, — coupé à intervalles réguliers par la crépitation des coups de feu d'un tir voisin, qui éclataient comme l'explosion des bouchons de champagne dans le bourdonnement d'une symphonie en sourdine.

Alors, sous le soleil qui lui chauffait le cerveau et dans l'atmosphère des ardents parfums de la Mort, il entendit une voix chuchoter sous la tombe où il s'était assis. Et cette voix disait: "Maudites soient vos cibles et vos carabines, turbulents vivants, qui vous souciez si peu des défunts et de leur divin repos! Maudites soient vos ambitions, maudits soient vos calculs, mortels impatients, qui venez étudier l'art de tuer auprès du sanctuaire de la Mort! Si vous saviez comme le prix est facile à gagner, comme le but est facile à toucher, et combien tout est néant, excepté la Mort, vous ne vous fatigueriez pas tant, laborieux vivants, et vous troubleriez moins souvent le sommeil de ceux qui depuis longtemps ont mis dans le But, dans le seul vrai but de la détestable vie!"

THE SHOOTING-RANGE AND THE CEMETERY

"Cemetery View Inn" – "A queer sign," said our traveller to himself; "but it raises a thirst! Certainly the keeper of this inn appreciates Horace and the poet pupils of Epicurus. Perhaps he even apprehends the profound philosophy of those old Egyptians who had no feast without its skeleton, or some emblem of life's brevity."

He entered: drank a glass of beer in presence of the tombs; and slowly smoked a cigar. Then, his phantasy driving him, he went down into the cemetery, where the grass was so tall and inviting; so brilliant in the sunshine.

The light and heat, indeed, were so furiously intense that one had said the drunken sun wallowed upon a carpet of flowers that had fattened upon the corruption beneath.

The air was heavy with vivid rumours of life – the life of things infinitely small – and broken at intervals by the crackling of shots from a neighbouring shooting-range, that exploded with a sound as of champagne corks to the burden of a hollow symphony.

And then, beneath a sun which scorched the brain, and in that atmosphere charged with the ardent perfume of death, he heard a voice whispering out of the tomb where he sat. And this voice said: "Accursed be your rifles and targets, you turbulent living ones, who care so little for the dead in their divine repose! Accursed be your ambitions and calculations, importunate mortals who study the arts of slaughter near the sanctuary of Death himself! Did you but know how easy the prize to win, how facile the end to reach, and how all save Death is naught, not so greatly would you fatigue yourselves, O ye laborious alive; nor would you so often vex the slumber of them that long ago reached the End – the only true end of life detestable!"

LE DÉSIR DE PEINDRE

Malheureux peut-être l'homme, mais heureux l'artiste que le désir déchire!

Je brûle de peindre celle qui m'est apparue si rarement et qui a fui si vite, comme une belle chose regrettable derrière le voyageur emporté dans la nuit. Comme il y a longtemps déjà qu'elle a disparu!

Elle est belle, et plus belle; elle est surprenante. En elle le noir abonde: et tout ce qu'elle inspire est nocturne et profond. Ses yeux sont deux antres où scintille vaguement le mystère, et son regard illumine comme l'éclair: c'est une explosion dans les ténèbres.

Je la comparerais à un soleil noir, si l'on pouvait concevoir un astre noir versant la lumière et le bonheur. Mais elle fait plus volontiers penser à la lune, qui sans doute l'a marquée de sa redoutable influence; non pas la lune blanche des idylles, qui ressemble à une froide mariée, mais la lune sinistre et enivrante, suspendue au fond d'une nuit orageuse et bousculée par les nuées qui courent; non pas la lune paisible et discrète visitant le sommeil des hommes purs, mais la lune arrachée du ciel, vaincue et révoltée, que les Sorcières thessaliennes contraignent durement à danser sur l'herbe terrifiée!

Dans son petit front habitent la volonté tenace et l'amour de la proie. Cependant, au bas de ce visage inquiétant, où des narines mobiles aspirent l'inconnu et l'impossible, éclate, avec une grâce inexprimable, le rire d'une grande bouche, rouge et blanche, et délicieuse, qui fait rêver au miracle d'une superbe fleur éclose dans un terrain volcanique.

Il y a des femmes qui inspirent l'envie de les vaincre et de jouir d'elles; mais celle-ci donne le désir de mourir lentement sous son regard.

THE DESIRE TO PAINT

Unhappy perhaps is the man, but happy the artist, who is torn with this desire.

I burn to paint a certain woman who has appeared to me so rarely, and so swiftly fled away, like some beautiful, regrettable thing the traveller must leave behind him in the night. It is already long since I saw her.

She is beautiful, and more than beautiful: she is overpowering. The colour black preponderates in her; all that she inspires is nocturnal and profound. Her eyes are two caverns where mystery vaguely stirs and gleams; her glance illuminates like a ray of light; it is an explosion in the darkness.

I would compare her to a black sun if one could conceive of a dark star overthrowing light and happiness. But it is the moon that she makes one dream of most readily; the moon, who has without doubt touched her with her own influence; not the white moon of the idylls, who resembles a cold bride, but the sinister and intoxicating moon suspended in the depths of a stormy night, among the driven clouds; not the discreet peaceful moon who visits the dreams of pure men, but the moon torn from the sky, conquered and revolted, that the witches of Thessaly hardly constrain to dance upon the terrified grass.

Her small brow is the habitation of a tenacious will and the love of prey. And below this inquiet face, whose mobile nostrils breathe in the unknown and the impossible, glitters, with an unspeakable grace, the smile of a large mouth; white, red, and delicious; a mouth that makes one dream of the miracle of some superb flower unclosing in a volcanic land.

There are women who inspire one with the desire to woo them and win them; but she makes one wish to die slowly beneath her steady gaze.

LE MAUVAIS VITRIER

Il y a des natures purement contemplatives et tout à fait impropres à l'action, qui cependant, sous une impulsion mystérieuse et inconnue, agissent quelquefois avec une rapidité dont elles se seraient crues elles-mêmes incapables.

Tel qui, craignant de trouver chez son concierge une nouvelle chagrinante, rôde lâchement une heure devant sa porte sans oser rentrer, tel qui garde quinze jours un lettre sans la décacheter, ou ne se résigne qu'au bout de six mois à opérer une démarche nécessaire depuis un an, se sentent quelquefois brusquement précipités vers l'action par une force irrésistible, comme la flèche d'un arc. Le moraliste et le médecin, qui prétendent tout savoir, ne peuvent pas expliquer d'où vient si subitement une si folle énergie à ces âmes paresseuses et voluptueuses, et comment, incapables d'accomplir les choses les plus simples et les plus nécessaires, elles trouvent à une certaine minute un courage de luxe pour exécuter les actes les plus absurdes et souvent même les plus dangereux.

Un de mes amis, le plus inoffensif rêveur qui ait existé, a mis une fois le feu à une forêt pour voir, disait-il, si le feu prenait avec autant de facilité qu'on l'affirme généralement. Dix fois de suite, l'expérience manqua; mais, à la onzième, elle réussit beaucoup trop bien.

Un autre allumera un cigare à côté d'un tonneau de poudre, pour voir, pour savoir, pour tenter la destinée, pour se contraindre lui-même à faire preuve d'énergie, pour faire le joueur, pour connaître les plaisirs de l'anxiété, pour rien, par caprice, par désœuvrement.

C'est une espèce d'énergie qui jaillit de l'ennui et de la rêverie; et ceux en qui elle se manifeste si inopinément sont, en général, comme je l'ai dit, les plus indolents et les plus rêveurs des êtres.

Un autre, timide à ce point qu'il baisse les yeux même devant les regards des hommes, à ce point qu'il lui faut rassembler toute sa pauvre volonté pour entrer dans un café ou passer devant le bureau d'un théâtre, où les contrôleurs lui paraissent investis de la majesté de Minos, d'Eaque et de Rhadamanthe, sautera brusquement au cou d'un vieillard qui passe à côté de lui et l'embrassera avec enthousiasme devant la foule étonnée.

Pourquoi? Parce que... parce que cette physionomie lui était irrésistiblement sympathique? Peut-être; mais il est plus légitime de supposer que lui-même il ne sait pas pourquoi.

J'ai été plus d'une fois victime de ces crises et de ces élans, qui nous autorisent à croire que des Démons malicieux se glissent en nous et nous font accomplir, à notre insu, leurs plus absurdes volontés.

Un matin je m'étais levé maussade, triste, fatigué d'oisiveté, et poussé, me semblait-il, à faire quelque chose de grand, une action d'éclat; et j'ouvris la fenêtre, hélas!

(Observez, je vous prie, que l'esprit de mystification qui, chez quelques personnes, n'est pas le résultat d'un travail ou d'une combinaison, mais d'une inspiration fortuite, participe beaucoup, ne fût-ce que par l'ardeur du désir, de cette humeur, hystérique selon les médecins, satanique selon ceux qui pensent un peu mieux que les médecins, qui nous pousse sans résistance vers une foule d'actions dangereuses ou inconvenantes.)

La première personne que j'aperçus dans la rue, ce fut un vitrier dont le cri perçant, discordant, monta jusqu'à moi à travers la lourde et sale atmosphère parisienne. Il me serait d'ailleurs impossible de dire pourquoi je fus pris à l'égard de ce pauvre homme d'une haine aussi soudaine que despotique.

" — Hé! hé!" et je lui criai de monter. Cependant je réfléchissais, non sans quelque gaieté, que, la chambre étant au sixième étage et l'escalier fort étroit, l'homme devait éprouver quelque peine à opérer son ascension et accrocher en maint endroit les angles de sa fragile marchandise.

Enfin il parut: j'examinai curieusement toutes ses vitres, et je lui dis: " — Comment? vous n'avez pas de verres de couleur? des verres roses, rouges, bleus, des vitres magiques, des vitres de paradis? Impudent que vous êtes! vous osez vous promener dans des quartiers pauvres, et vous n'avez pas même de vitres qui fassent voir la vie en beau!" Et je le poussai vivement vers l'escalier, où il trébucha en grognant.

Je m'approchai du balcon et je me saisis d'un petit pot de fleurs, et quand l'homme reparut au débouché de la porte, je laissai tomber perpendiculairement mon engin de guerre sur le rebord postérieur de ses crochets; et le choc le renversant, il acheva de briser sous son dos toute sa pauvre fortune ambulatoire qui rendit le bruit éclatant d'un palais de cristal crevé par la foudre.

Et, ivre de ma folie, je lui criai furieusement: "La vie en beau! la vie en beau!"

Ces plaisanteries nerveuses ne sont pas sans péril, et on peut souvent les payer cher. Mais qu'importe l'éternité de la damnation à qui a trouvé dans une seconde l'infini de la jouissance?

THE GLASS-VENDOR

These are some natures purely contemplative and antipathetic to action, who nevertheless, under a mysterious and inexplicable impulse, sometimes act with a rapidity of which they would have believed themselves incapable. Such a one is he who, fearing to find some new vexation awaiting him at his lodgings, prowls about in a cowardly fashion before the door without daring to enter; such a one is he who keeps a letter fifteen days without opening it, or only makes up his mind at the end of six months to undertake a journey that has been a necessity for a year past. Such beings sometimes feel themselves precipitately thrust towards action, like an arrow from a bow.

The novelist and the physician, who profess to know all things, yet cannot explain whence comes this sudden and delirious energy to indolent and voluptuous souls; nor how, incapable of accomplishing the simplest and most necessary things, they are at some certain moment of time possessed by a superabundant hardihood which enables them to execute the most absurd and even the most dangerous acts.

One of my friends, the most harmless dreamer that ever lived, at one time set fire to a forest, in order to ascertain, as he said, whether the flames take hold with the easiness that is commonly affirmed. His experiment failed ten times running, on the eleventh it succeeded only too well.

Another lit a cigar by the side of a powder barrel, *in order to see, to know, to tempt Destiny*, for a jest, to have the pleasure of suspense, for no reason at all, out of caprice, out of idleness. This is a kind of energy that springs from weariness and reverie; and those in whom it manifests so stubbornly are in general, as I have said, the most indolent and dreamy beings.

Another so timid that he must cast down his eyes before the gaze of any man, and summon all his poor will before he dare enter a café or pass the pay-box of a theatre, where the ticket-seller seems, in his eyes, invested with all the majesty of Minos, Æcus, and Rhadamanthus, will at times throw himself upon the neck of some old man whom he sees in the street, and embrace him with enthusiasm in sight of an astonished crowd. Why? Because – because this countenance is irresistibly attractive to him? Perhaps; but it is more legitimate to suppose that he himself does not know why.

I have been more than once a victim to these crises and outbreaks which give us cause to believe that evil-meaning demons slip into us, to make us the ignorant accomplices of their most absurd desires. One morning I arose in a sullen mood, very sad, and tired of idleness, and thrust as it seemed to me to the doing of some great thing, some brilliant act – and then, alas, I opened the window.

(I beg you to observe that in some people the spirit of mystification is not the result of labour or combination, but rather of a fortuitous inspiration which would partake, were it not for the strength of the feeling, of the mood called hysterical by the physician and satanic by those who think a little more profoundly than the physician; the mood which thrusts us unresisting to a multitude of dangerous and inconvenient acts.)

The first person I noticed in the street was a glass-vendor whose shrill and discordant cry mounted up to me through the heavy, dull atmosphere of Paris. It would have been else impossible to account for the sudden and despotic hatred of this poor man that came upon me.

"Hello, there!" I cried, and bade him ascend. Meanwhile I reflected, not without gaiety, that as my room was on the sixth landing, and the stairway very narrow, the man would have some difficulty in ascending, and in many a place would break off the corners of his fragile merchandise.

At length he appeared. I examined all his glasses with curiosity, and then said to him: "What, have you no coloured glasses? Glasses of rose and crimson and blue, magical glasses, glasses of Paradise? You are insolent. You dare to walk in mean streets when you have no glasses that would make one see beauty in life?" And I hurried him briskly to the staircase, which he staggered down, grumbling.

I went on to the balcony and caught up a little flower-pot, and when the man appeared in the door-way beneath I let fall my engine of war perpendicularly upon the edge of his pack, so that it was upset by the shock and all his poor walking fortune broken to bits. It made a noise like a palace of crystal shattered by lightning. Mad with my folly, I cried furiously after him: "The life beautiful! the life beautiful!"

Such nervous pleasantries are not without peril; often enough one pays dearly for them. But what matters an eternity of damnation to him who has found in one second an eternity of enjoyment?

LES VEUVES

Vauvenargues dit que dans les jardins publics il est des allées hantées principalement par l'ambition déçue, par les inventeurs malheureux, par les gloires avortées, par les coeurs brisés, par toutes ces âmes tumultueuses et fermées, en qui grondent encore les derniers soupirs d'un orage et qui reculent loin du regard insolent des joyeux et des oisifs. Ces retraites ombreuses sont les rendez-vous des éclopés de la vie.

C'est surtout vers ces lieux que le poëte et le philosophe aiment diriger leurs avides conjectures. Il y a là une pâture certaine. Car s'il est une place qu'ils dédaignent de visiter, comme je l'insinuais tout à l'heure, c'est surtout la joie des riches. Cette turbulence dans le vide n'a rien qui les attire. Au contraire, ils se sentent irrésistiblement entraînés vers tout ce qui est faible, ruiné, contristé, orphelin.

Un oeil expérimenté ne s'y trompe jamais. Dans ces traits rigides ou abattus, dans ces yeux caves et ternes, ou brillants des derniers éclairs de la lutte, dans ces rides profondes et nombreuses, dans ces démarches si lentes ou si saccadées, il déchiffre tout de suite les innombrables légendes de l'amour trompé, du dévouement méconnu, des efforts non récompensés, de la faim et du froid humblement, silencieusement supportés.

Avez-vous quelquefois aperçu des veuves sur ces bancs solitaires, des veuves pauvres? Qu'elles soient en deuil ou non, il est facile de les reconnaître. D'ailleurs il y a toujours dans le deuil du pauvre quelque chose qui manque, une absence d'harmonie qui le rend plus navrant. Il est contraint de lésiner sur sa douleur. Le riche porte la sienne au grand complet.

Quelle est la veuve la plus triste et la plus attristante, celle qui traîne à sa main un bambin avec qui elle ne peut pas partager sa rêverie, ou celle qui est tout à fait seule? Je ne sais... Il m'est arrivé une fois de suivre pendant de longues heures une vieille affligée de cette espèce; celle-là roide, droite, sous un petit châle usé, portait dans tout son être une fierté de stoïcienne.

Elle était évidemment condamnée, par une absolue solitude, à des habitudes de vieux célibataire, et le caractère masculin de ses mœurs ajoutait un piquant mystérieux à leur austérité. Je ne sais dans quel misérable café et de quelle façon elle déjeuna. Je la suivis au cabinet de lecture; et je l'épiai longtemps pendant qu'elle cherchait dans les gazettes, avec des yeux actifs, jadis brûlés par les larmes, des nouvelles d'un intérêt puissant et personnel.

Enfin, dans l'après-midi, sous un ciel d'automne charmant, un de ces ciels d'où descendent en foule les regrets et les souvenirs, elle s'assit à l'écart dans un jardin, pour entendre, loin de la foule, un de ces concerts dont la musique des régiments gratifie le peuple parisien.

C'était sans doute là la petite débauche de cette vieille innocente (ou de cette vieille purifiée), la consolation bien gagnée d'une de ces lourdes journées sans ami, sans causerie, sans joie, sans confident, que Dieu laissait tomber sur elle, depuis bien des ans peut-être! trois cent soixante-cinq fois par an.

Une autre encore:

Je ne puis jamais m'empêcher de jeter un regard, sinon universellement sympathique, au moins curieux, sur la foule de parias qui se pressent autour de l'enceinte d'un concert public. L'orchestre jette à travers la nuit des chants de fête, de triomphe ou de volupté. Les robes traînent en miroitant; les regards se croisent; les oisifs, fatigués de n'avoir rien fait, se dandinent, feignant de déguster indolemment la musique. Ici rien que de riche, d'heureux; rien qui ne respire et n'inspire l'insouciance et le plaisir de se laisser vivre; rien, excepté l'aspect de cette tourbe qui s'appuie là-bas sur la barrière extérieure, attrapant gratis, au gré du vent, un lambeau de musique, et regardant l'étincelante fournaise intérieure. C'est toujours chose intéressante que ce reflet de la joie du riche au fond de l'oeil du pauvre. Mais ce jour-là, à travers ce peuple vêtu de blouses et d'indienne, j'aperçus un être dont la noblesse faisait un éclatant contraste avec toute la trivialité environnante.

C'était une femme grande, majestueuse, et si noble dans tout son air, que je n'ai pas souvenir d'avoir vu sa pareille dans les collections des aristocratiques beautés du passé. Un parfum de hautaine vertu émanait de toute sa personne. Son visage, triste et amaigri, était en parfaite accordance avec le grand deuil dont elle était revêtue. Elle aussi, comme la plèbe à laquelle elle s'était mêlée et qu'elle ne voyait pas, elle regardait le monde lumineux avec un oeil profond, et elle écoutait en hochant doucement la tête.

Singulière vision! "A coup sûr, me dis-je, cette pauvreté-là, si pauvreté il y a, ne doit pas admettre l'économie sordide; un si noble visage m'en répond. Pourquoi donc reste-t-elle volontairement dans un milieu où elle fait une tache si éclatante?"

Mais en passant curieusement auprès d'elle, je crus en deviner la raison. La grande veuve tenait par la main un enfant comme elle vêtu de noir; si modique que fût le prix d'entrée, ce prix suffisait peut-être pour payer un des besoins du petit être, mieux encore, une superfluité, un jouet.

Et elle sera rentrée à pied, méditant et rêvant, seule, toujours seule; car l'enfant est turbulent, égoïste, sans douceur et sans patience; et il ne peut même pas, comme le pur animal, comme le chien et le chat, servir de confident aux douleurs solitaires.

THE WIDOWS

Vauvenargues says that in public gardens there are alleys haunted principally by thwarted ambition, by unfortunate inventors, by aborted glories and broken hearts, and by all those tumultuous and contracted souls in whom the last sighs of the storm mutter yet again, and who thus betake themselves far from the insolent and joyous eyes of the well-to-do. These shadowy retreats are the rendezvous of life's cripples.

To such places above all others do the poet and philosopher direct their avid conjectures. They find there an unfailing pasturage, for if there is one place they disdain to visit it is, as I have already hinted, the place of the joy of the rich. A turmoil in the void has no attractions for them. On the contrary they feel themselves irresistibly drawn towards all that is feeble, ruined, sorrowing, and bereft.

An experienced eye is never deceived. In these rigid and dejected lineaments; in these eyes, wan and hollow, or bright with the last fading gleams of the combat against fate; in these numerous profound wrinkles and in the slow and troubled gait, the eye of experience deciphers unnumbered legends of mistaken devotion, of unrewarded effort, of hunger and cold humbly and silently supported.

Have you not at times seen widows sitting on the deserted benches? Poor widows, I mean. Whether in mourning or not they are easily recognised. Moreover, there is always something wanting in the mourning of the poor; a lack of harmony which but renders it the more heart-breaking. It is forced to be niggardly in its show of grief. They are the rich who exhibit a full complement of sorrow.

Who is the saddest and most saddening of widows: she who leads by the hand a child who cannot share her reveries, or she who is quite alone? I do not know.... It happened that I once followed for several long hours an aged and afflicted woman of this kind: rigid and erect, wrapped in a little worn shawl, she carried in all her being the pride of stoicism.

She was evidently condemned by her absolute loneliness to the habits of an ancient celibacy; and the masculine characters of her habits added to their austerity a piquant mysteriousness. In what miserable café she dines I know not, nor in what manner. I followed her to a reading-room, and for a long time watched her reading the papers, her active eyes, that once burned with tears, seeking for news of a powerful and personal interest.

At length, in the afternoon, under a charming autumnal sky, one of those skies that let fall hosts of memories and regrets, she seated herself remotely in a garden, to listen, far from the crowd, to one of the regimental bands whose music gratifies the people of Paris. This was without doubt the small debauch of the innocent old woman (or the purified old woman), the well-earned consolation for another of the burdensome days without a friend, without conversation, without joy, without a confidant, that God had allowed to fall upon her perhaps for many years past – three hundred and sixty-five times a year!

Yet one more:

I can never prevent myself from throwing a glance, if not sympathetic at least full of curiosity, over the crowd of outcasts who press around the enclosure of a public concert. From the orchestra, across the night, float songs of fête, of triumph, or of pleasure. The dresses of the women sweep and shimmer; glances pass; the well-to-do, tired with doing nothing, saunter about and make indolent pretence of listening to the music. Here are only the rich, the happy; here is nothing that does not inspire or exhale the pleasure of being alive, except the aspect of the mob that presses against the outer barrier yonder, catching gratis, at the will of the wind, a tatter of music, and watching the glittering furnace within.

There is a reflection of the joy of the rich deep in the eyes of the poor that is always interesting. But to-day, beyond this people dressed in blouses and calico, I saw one whose nobility was in striking contrast with all the surrounding triviality. She was a tall, majestic woman, and so imperious in all her air that I cannot remember having seen the like in the collections of the aristocratic beauties of the past. A perfume of exalted virtue emanated from all her being. Her face, sad and worn, was in perfect keeping with the deep mourning in which she was dressed. She also, like the plebeians she mingled with and did not see, looked upon the luminous world with a profound eye, and listened with a toss of her head.

It was a strange vision. "Most certainly," I said to myself, "this poverty, if poverty it be, ought not to admit of any sordid economy; so noble a face answers for that. Why then does she remain in surroundings with which she is so strikingly in contrast?"

But in curiously passing near her I was able to divine the reason. The tall widow held by the hand a child dressed like herself in black. Modest as was the price of entry, this price perhaps sufficed to pay for some of the needs of the little being, or even more, for a superfluity, a toy.

She will return on foot, dreaming and meditating – and alone, always alone, for the child is turbulent and selfish, without gentleness or patience, and cannot become, any more than another animal, a dog or a cat, the confidant of solitary griefs.

LES TENTATIONS OU ÉROS, PLUTUS ET LA GLOIRE

Deux superbes Satans et une Diablesse, non moins extraordinaire, ont la nuit dernière monté l'escalier mystérieux par où l'Enfer donne assaut à la faiblesse de l'homme qui dort, et communique en secret avec lui. Et ils sont venus se poser glorieusement devant moi, debout comme sur une estrade. Une splendeur sulfureuse émanait de ces trois personnages, qui se détachaient ainsi du fond opaque de la nuit. Ils avaient l'air si fier et si plein de domination, que je les pris d'abord tous les trois pour de vrais Dieux.

Le visage du premier Satan était d'un sexe ambigu, et il avait aussi, dans les lignes de son corps, la mollesse des anciens Bacchus. Ses beaux yeux languissants, d'une couleur ténébreuse et indécise, ressemblaient à des violettes chargées encore des lourds pleurs de l'orage, et ses lèvres entr'ouvertes à des cassolettes chaudes, d'où s'exhalait la bonne odeur d'une parfumerie; et à chaque fois qu'il soupirait, des insectes musqués s'illuminaient, en voletant, aux ardeurs de son souffle.

Autour de sa tunique de pourpre était roulé, en manière de ceinture, un serpent chatoyant qui, la tête relevée, tournait langoureusement vers lui ses yeux de braise. A cette ceinture vivante étaient suspendus, alternant avec des fioles pleines de liqueurs sinistres, de brillants couteaux et des instruments de chirurgie. Dans sa main droite il tenait une autre fiole dont le contenu était d'un rouge lumineux, et qui portait pour étiquette ces mots bizarres: "Buvez, ceci est mon sang, un parfait cordial..." dans la gauche, un violon qui lui servait sans doute à chanter ses plaisirs et ses douleurs, et à répandre la contagion de sa folie dans les nuits de sabbat.

A ses chevilles délicates traînaient quelques anneaux d'une chaîne d'or rompue, et quand la gêne qui en résultait le forçait à baisser les yeux vers la terre, il contemplait vaniteusement les ongles de ses pieds, brillants et polis comme des pierres bien travaillées.

Il me regarda avec ses yeux inconsolablement navrés, d'où s'écoulait une insidieuse ivresse, et il me dit d'une voix chantante: "Si tu veux, si tu veux, je te ferai le seigneur des âmes, et tu seras le maître de la matière vivante, plus encore que le sculpteur peut l'être de l'argile; et tu connaîtras le plaisir, sans cesse renaissant, de sortir de toi-même pour t'oublier dans autrui, et d'attirer les autres âmes jusqu'à les confondre avec la tienne."

Et je lui répondis: "Grand merci! je n'ai que faire de cette pacotille d'êtres qui, sans doute, ne valent pas mieux que mon pauvre moi. Bien que j'aie quelque honte à me souvenir, je ne veux rien oublier; et quand même je ne connaîtrais pas, vieux monstre, ta mystérieuse coutellerie, tes fioles équivoques, les chaînes dont tes pieds sont empêtrés, sont des symboles qui expliquent assez clairement les inconvénients de ton amitié. Garde tes présents."

Le second Satan n'avait ni cet air à la fois tragique et souriant, ni ces belles manières insinuantes, ni cette beauté délicate et parfumée. C'était un homme vaste, à gros visage sans yeux, dont la lourde bedaine surplombait les cuisses, et dont toute la peau était dorée et illustrée, comme d'un tatouage, d'une foule de petites figures mouvantes représentant les formes nombreuses de la misère universelle. Il y avait de petits hommes efflanqués qui se suspendaient volontairement à un clou; il y avait de petits gnomes difformes, maigres, dont les yeux suppliants réclamaient l'aumône mieux encore que leurs mains tremblantes; et puis de vieilles mères portant des avortons accrochés à leurs mamelles exténuées. Il y en avait encore bien d'autres.

Le gros Satan tapait avec son poing sur son immense ventre, d'où sortait alors un long et retentissant cliquetis de métal qui se terminait en un vague gémissement fait de nombreuses voix humaines. Et il riait, en montrant impudemment ses dents gâtées, d'un énorme rire imbécile, comme certains hommes de tous les pays quand ils ont trop bien dîné.

Et celui-là me dit: "Je puis te donner ce qui obtient tout, ce qui vaut tout, ce qui remplace tout!" Et il tapa sur son ventre monstrueux, dont l'écho sonore fit le commentaire de sa grossière parole.

Je me détournai avec dégoût, et je répondis: "Je n'ai besoin, pour ma jouissance, de la misère de personne; et je ne veux pas d'une richesse attristée, comme un papier de tenture, de tous les malheurs représentés sur ta peau."

Quant à la Diablesse, je mentirais si je n'avouais pas qu'à première vue je lui trouvai un bizarre charme. Pour définir ce charme, je ne saurais le comparer à rien de mieux qu'à celui des très-belles femmes sur le retour, qui cependant ne vieillissent plus, et dont la beauté garde la magie pénétrante des ruines. Elle avait l'air à la fois impérieux et dégingandé, et ses yeux, quoique battus, contenaient une force fascinatrice. Ce qui me frappa le plus, ce fut le mystère de sa voix, dans laquelle je retrouvais le souvenir des *contralti* les plus délicieux et aussi un peu de l'enrouement des gosiers incessamment lavés par l'eau-de-vie.

"Veux-tu connaître ma puissance?" dit la fausse déesse avec sa voix charmante et paradoxale. "Ecoute."

Et elle emboucha alors une gigantesque trompette, enrubannée, comme un mirliton, des titres de tous les journaux de l'univers, et à travers cette trompette elle cria mon nom, qui roula ainsi à travers l'espace avec le bruit de cent mille tonnerres, et me revint répercuté par l'écho de la plus lointaine planète.

"Diable!" fis-je, à moitié subjugué, "voilà qui est précieux!" Mais en examinant plus attentivement la séduisante virago, il me sembla vaguement que je la reconnaissais pour l'avoir vue trinquant avec quelques drôles de ma connaissance; et le son rauque du cuivre apporta à mes oreilles je ne sais quel souvenir d'une trompette prostituée.

Aussi je répondis, avec tout mon dédain: "Va-t'en! Je ne suis pas fait pour épouser la maîtresse de certains que je ne veux pas nommer."

Certes, d'une si courageuse abnégation j'avais le droit d'être fier Mais malheureusement je me réveillai, et toute ma force m'abandonna. "En vérité, me dis-je, il fallait que je fusse bien lourdement assoupi pour montrer de tels scrupules. Ah! s'ils pouvaient revenir pendant que je suis éveillé, je ne ferais pas tant le délicat!"

Et je les invoquai à haute voix, les suppliant de me pardonner, leur offrant de me déshonorer aussi souvent qu'il le faudrait pour mériter leurs faveurs; mais je les avais sans doute fortement offensés, car ils ne sont jamais revenus.

THE TEMPTATIONS; OR, EROS, PLUTUS, AND GLORY

Last night two superb Satans and a She-devil not less extraordinary ascended the mysterious stairway by which Hell gains access to the frailty of sleeping man, and communes with him in secret. These three postured gloriously before me, as though they had been upon a stage – and a sulphurous splendour emanated from these beings who so disengaged themselves from the opaque heart of the night. They bore with them so proud a presence, and so full of mastery, that at first I took them for three of the true Gods.

The first Satan, by his face, was a creature of doubtful sex. The softness of an ancient Bacchus shone in the lines of his body. His beautiful langourous eyes, of a tenebrous and indefinite colour, were like violets still laden with the heavy tears of the storm; his slightly-parted lips were like heated censers, from whence exhaled the sweet savour of many perfumes; and each time he breathed, exotic insects drew, as they fluttered, strength from the ardours of his breath.

Twined about his tunic of purple stuff, in the manner of a cincture, was an iridescent Serpent with lifted head and eyes like embers turned sleepily towards him. Phials full of sinister fluids, alternating with shining knives and instruments of surgery, hung from this living girdle. He held in his right hand a flagon containing a luminous red fluid, and inscribed with a legend in these singular words:

"DRINK OF THIS MY BLOOD: A PERFECT RESTORATIVE";

and in his left hand held a violin that without doubt served to sing his pleasures and pains, and to spread abroad the contagion of his folly upon the nights of the Sabbath.

From rings upon his delicate ankles trailed a broken chain of gold, and when the burden of this caused him to bend his eyes towards the earth, he would contemplate with vanity the nails of his feet, as brilliant and polished as well-wrought jewels.

He looked at me with eyes inconsolably heartbroken and giving forth an insidious intoxication, and cried in a chanting voice: "If thou wilt, if thou wilt, I will make thee an overlord of souls; thou shalt be master of living matter more perfectly than the sculptor is master of his clay; thou shalt taste the pleasure, reborn without end, of obliterating thyself in the self of another, and of luring other souls to lose themselves in thine."

But I replied to him: "I thank thee. I only gain from this venture, then, beings of no more worth than my poor self? Though remembrance brings me shame indeed, I would forget nothing; and even before I recognised thee, thou ancient monster, thy mysterious cutlery, thy equivocal phials, and the chain that imprisons thy feet, were symbols showing clearly enough the inconvenience of thy friendship. Keep thy gifts."

The second Satan had neither the air at once tragical and smiling, the lovely insinuating ways, nor the delicate and scented beauty of the first. A gigantic man, with a coarse, eyeless face, his heavy paunch overhung his hips and was gilded and pictured, like a tattooing, with a crowd of little moving figures which represented the unnumbered forms of universal misery. There were little sinew-shrunken men who hung themselves willingly from nails; there were meagre gnomes, deformed and under-sized, whose beseeching eyes begged an alms even more eloquently than their trembling hands; there were old mothers who nursed clinging abortions at their pendent breasts. And many others, even more surprising.

This heavy Satan beat with his fist upon his immense belly, from whence came a loud and resounding metallic clangour, which died away in a sighing made by many human voices. And he smiled unrestrainedly, showing his broken teeth – the imbecile smile of a man who has dined too freely. Then the creature said to me:

"I can give thee that which gets all, which is worth all, which takes the place of all." And he tapped his monstrous paunch, whence came a sonorous echo as the commentary to his obscene speech. I turned away with disgust and replied: "I need no man's misery to bring me happiness; nor will I have the sad wealth of all the misfortunes pictured upon thy skin as upon a tapestry."

As for the She-devil, I should lie if I denied that at first I found in her a certain strange charm, which to define I can but compare to the charm of certain beautiful women past their first youth, who yet seem to age no more, whose beauty keeps something of the penetrating magic of ruins. She had an air at once imperious and sordid, and her eyes, though heavy, held a certain power of fascination. I was struck most by her voice, wherein I found the remembrance of the most delicious contralti, as well as a little of the hoarseness of a throat continually laved with brandy.

"Wouldst thou know my power?" said the charming and paradoxical voice of the false goddess. "Then listen." And she put to her mouth a gigantic trumpet, enribboned, like a mirliton, with the titles of all the newspapers in the world; and through this trumpet she cried my name so that it rolled through space with the sound of a hundred thousand thunders, and came re-echoing back to me from the farthest planet.

"Devil!" cried I, half tempted, "that at least is worth something." But it vaguely struck me, upon examining the seductive virago more attentively, that I had seen her clinking glasses with certain drolls of my acquaintance, and her blare of brass carried to my ears I know not what memory of a fanfare prostituted.

So I replied, with all disdain: "Get thee hence! I know better than wed the light o' love of them that I will not name."

Truly, I had the right to be proud of a so courageous renunciation. But unfortunately I awoke, and all my courage left me. "In truth," I said, "I must have been very deeply asleep indeed to have had such scruples. Ah, if they would but return while I am awake, I would not be so delicate."

So I invoked the three in a loud voice, offering to dishonour myself as often as necessary to obtain their favours; but I had without doubt too deeply offended them, for they have never returned.

A NOTE ON CHARLES BAUDELAIRE

By Jeremy Mark Robinson

Charles Baudelaire (Apl 9, 1821, Paris - Aug 31, 1867, Paris) is one of the great, 19th century French poets, part of the group that includes Paul Verlaine, Lautréamont, Gérard de Nerval and Arthur Rimbaud. Baudelaire is a poet's poet – a poet who enshrines the act and consumption of poetry, a poet who is worth studying in detail, and a poet who provides everything you might wish for: precise technical qualities, soaring lyricism, a unique vision, grand themes, vivid cultural expressions of the era, and of course the bohemian/ decadent lifestyle.

Charles Baudelaire embodies many aspects of the mid-to-late 19th century culturally and politically, which he expressed in his poetry. Through Baudelaire you can connect to so many elements of 19th century French and European cultural life, including many of the key artists of the day, such as Delacroix, Balzac, Hugo, Wagner, Liszt, Manet, Gautier, Nadar, Poe, Courbet, Rops, Flaubert, Daumier and Champfleury (Baudelaire knew many of them, such as the photographer Félix Nadar, who photographed him, and the artists Edouard Manet and Gustave Courbet, who painted his portrait).

Charles Baudelaire's era was that of Symbolism and

Decadence, and the chief poets of Symbolism and Decadence included Arthur Rimbaud, Gérard de Nerval, Tristan Corbière, Stéphane Mallarmé, Lautréamont and Pauls Verlaine and Valéry. The Symbolist and Decadent age was marked by 'gory exoticism', as Mario Praz put it (289), by the æstheticism of 'beauty', opulence and indulgence, mysticism, black magic and the macabre, where the key phrase is from Paul Verlaine: 'Je suis l'Empire à la fin de la décadence', which he wrote in 1885 in a poem entitled (what else?) 'Langueur'.[1] The word, *decadence*, from Verlaine, connotes profuse amounts of eroticism, debauchery, declining state power, Imperialism and 'perversions'. But it was Baudelaire who really launched the Decadent poetic movement with his famous *Flowers of Evil* collection of poems.

Like other poets of the Symbolist era – Arthur Rimbaud, Stéphane Mallarmé, Théodore de Banville – Charles Baudelaire's poetry (as with Symbolism) exhibits many affinities with Romanticism: the pantheism and nature mysticism; the love of occultism, paganism, Hellenism, travel and exotica; the cult of the individual; the social rebellion; the exaltation of solitude; the sense of melancholy; the emphasis on subjective experience; the use of drugs and intoxicants; the urge to go to extremes; the leaning towards infinity, and so on.

Charles Baudelaire has proved to be as fascinating a poet in his personality and his life, which has coloured the critical reception of his work. He was a rock 'n' roll poet a hundred years before the rock 'n' roll way of life existed (as with Arthur Rimbaud). It's no surprise that Baudelaire's poetry has, like Rimbaud's, been influential on pop musicians, as well as being adapted for classical music (many pop acts have adapted Baudelaire's poems as song lyrics, drawing most of all on *Flowers of Evil*, inevitably).

Charles Baudelaire's lifestyle was famously bohemian, with suitably sleazy elements (such as drink, drugs (opium and

---

[1] P. Verlaine, *One Hundred and One Poems*, tr. N. Shapiro, University Press, Chicago, IL, 1999, 134.

laudanum), and prostitutes). He was plagued by money trouble throughout his life. One of his muses was the 'Black Venus', Jeanne Duval (celebrated in poems in *Flowers of Evil* such as 'To a Creole Lady' and 'The Balcony'), alongside Apollonie Sabatier the courtesan and Marie Daubrun the actress.

The Flowers of Evil was Charles Baudelaire's first book of poetry, published in 1857. Subsequent editions appeared in 1861 and 1868. Six poems were suppressed in editions after the first, 1857 edition on grounds of disrupting public morality (but appeared in other publications). *The Flowers of Evil* upset the conservative culture of the period, leading to prosecution for the poet and his publisher, Auguste Poulet Malassis (of Poulet-Malassis et de Broise).

Formally, Charles Baudelaire is a master craftsman, selecting challenging poetic forms such as the sonnet (many of Baudelaire's famous poems are sonnets: 'Correspondences', 'Exotic Perfume', 'Spleen', 'Beauty', etc). The Baudelaireian sonnet employs 14 lines split into two groups, of 8 and 6 lines, with a break after the eighth line. The rime scheme is typically abab, abab, ccd, ccd.

Another poetic form that Baudelaire took up and helped to popularize was the prose poem – a poem in prose form: 'Evening Twilight', 'The Eyes of the Poor', 'Venus and the Fool', 'Intoxication', etc. Arthur Rimbaud was influenced by Baudelaire's example, and produced his own prose poems.

Charles Baudelaire's influence has been enormous – poets influenced by him include Arthur Rimbaud, Stéphane Mallarmé, Paul Verlaine and T.S. Eliot, and writers such as Marcel Proust, J.-K. Huysmans, Lawrence Durrell, Walter Benjamin, and Edmund Wilson.

BIBLIOGRAPHY

CHARLES BAUDELAIRE

Oeuvres Complètes, 19 volumes, eds. J. Crépet & C. Pichois, Conrad, Paris, 1922-53
Prose and Poetry, tr. A. Symons, Boni & Liveright, 1926
Flowers of Evil. tr. G. Dillon & E. Millay, Harper, 1936
Paris, Spleen, tr. L. Varèse, New Directions, 1947
My Heart Laid Bare and Other Prose Writings, tr. N. Carmeron, Vanguard, 1951
The Voyage and Other Versions of Poems, tr. R. Lowell, Farrar, Straus & Giroux, 1961
Petits Poèms en Prose, Corti, Paris, 1969
Oeuvres Complètes, 2 vols, Gallimard, 1975-77
Les Fleurs du Mal, David Godine, 1983
The Parisian Prowler, tr. Ed. Kaplan, University of Georgia Press, 1989
Flowers of Evil and Other Works, tr. W. Fowlie, Dover, New York, 1992
The Flowers of Evil, tr. J. McGowan, Oxford University Press, 1993
Selected Poems, ed. C. Clark, Penguin, 1995
Baudelaire's Flowers of Evil, ed. L. Porter, Modern Language Association, 2000

OTHERS

N. Babuts. *Baudelaire*, University of Delaware Press, 1997
J. Bennett. *Baudelaire*, Princeton University Press, 1946
L. Bersani. *Baudelaire and Freud*, University of California Press, 1978
S. Blood. *Baudelaire and the Aesthetics of Bad Faith*, Stanford University Press, 1997
D. Carrier. *High Art: Charles Baudelaire and the Origins of Modernist*

Painting, Pennsylvania State University Press, 1996
G. Chesters. *Baudelaire and the Poetics of Craft*, Cambridge University Press, 1988
J. Coven. *Baudelaire's Voyages*, Bullfinch Press, 1993
E. Delahaye. *Souveniers familiers à propos de Rimbaud, Verlaine et Germain Nouveau*, Messein, 1925
P. Emmanuel. *Baudelaire*, University of Alabama Press, 1970
M. Evans. *Baudelaire and Intertextuality*, Cambridge University Press, 1993
M. Gilman. *Baudelaire the Critic*, 1943
M. Hannoosh. *Baudelaire and Caricature*, Pennsylvania State University Press, 1992
F. Hemmings. *Baudelaire the Damned*, Hamish Hamilton, 1982
J. Hiddleston. *Baudelaire and the Art of Memory*, Oxford University Press, 1999
E. Holland. *Baudelaire and Schizoanalysis*, Cambridge University Press, 1993
L. Hyslop. *Baudelaire*, Yale University Press, 1980
A. De Jonge. *Baudelaire*, Putnam, 1977
N. Jouve. *Baudelaire*, Palgrave Macmillan, 1980
J. Lawler. *Poetry and Moral Dialectic: Baudelaire "Secret Architecture"*, Farleigh Dickinson University Press, 1997
F. Leakey. *Baudelaire and Nature*, Manchester University Press, 1969
—. *Baudelaire*, Cambridge University Press, 1990
R. Lloyd. *Baudelaire's World*, Cornell University Press, 2002
J. MacInnes. *The Comical As Textual Practice In Les Fleurs Du Mal*, University Press of Florida, 1988
E. Morgan. *Flower of Evil: Life of Charles Baudelaire*, Ayer Co., 1943
H. Peyre, ed. *Baudelaire*, Prentice Hall, 1962
C. Pichois & J. Ziegler. *Baudelaire*, Viking Press, 1989
G. Poulet. *Exploding Poetry: Baudelaire, Rimbaud*, University of Chicago Press, 1984
Mario Praz: *The Romantic Agony*, tr. A. Davidson, Oxford University Press, Oxford, 1933
Joanna Richardson. *Verlaine*, Weidenfeld & Nicolson, London, 1971
—. *Baudelaire*, St Martin's Press, New York, 1994
George Stambolian & Elaine Marks, eds. *Homosexuality and French Literature: Cultural Contexts/ Critical Texts*, Cornell University Press, Ithaca, 1979
E, Starkie. *Baudelaire*, New Directions, 1958
W.J. Thompson. *Understanding Les Fleurs du Mal*, Vanderbilt Universityfi Press, Nashville, 1997
P. Ward & J. Patty, eds. *Baudelaire and the Poetics of Modernity*, Vanderbilt University Press, 2001

In the Dim Void

Samuel Beckett's Late Trilogy: *Company, Ill Seen, Ill Said* and *Worstward Ho*

by Gregory Johns

This book discusses the luminous beauty and dense, rigorous poetry of Samuel Beckett's late works, *Company, Ill Seen, Ill Said* and *Worstward Ho*. Gregory Johns looks back over Beckett's long writing career, charting the development from the *Molloy-Malone Dies-Unnamable* trilogy through the 'fizzles' of the 1960s to the elegiac lyricism of the *Company* series. Johns compares the trilogy with late plays such as *Ghosts, Footfalls* and *Rockaby*.

Bibliography, notes. Illustrated. 120pp
ISBN 9781861712974 Pbk and ISBN 9781861712608 Hbk
9781861713407 E-book

Beauties, Beasts, and Enchantment

CLASSIC FRENCH FAIRY TALES

Translated and with an Introduction
by Jack Zipes

A collection of 36 classic French fairy tales translated by renowned writer Jack Zipes. *Cinderella, Beauty and the Beast, Sleeping Beauty* and *Little Red Riding Hood* are among the classic fairy tales in this amazing book.
Includes illustrations from fairy tale collections.
Jack Zipes has written and published widely on fairy tales.

'Terrific... a succulent array of 17th and 18th century 'salon' fairy tales'
- *The New York Times Book Review*

'These tales are adventurous, thrilling in a way fairy tales are meant to be... The translation from the French is modern, happily free of archaic and hyperbolic language... a fine and sophisticated collection' - *New York Tribune*

'Enjoyable to read... a unique collection of French regional folklore' - *Library Journal*

'Charming stories accompanied by attractive pen-and-ink drawings' - *Chattanooga Times*

Introduction and illustrations   612pp.   ISBN 9781861712510 Pbk   ISBN 9781861713193 Hbk

CRESCENT MOON PUBLISHING

web: www.crmoon.com e-mail: cresmopub@yahoo.co.uk

ARTS, PAINTING, SCULPTURE

The Art of Andy Goldsworthy
Andy Goldsworthy: Touching Nature
Andy Goldsworthy in Close-Up
Andy Goldsworthy: Pocket Guide
Andy Goldsworthy In America
Land Art: A Complete Guide
The Art of Richard Long
Richard Long: Pocket Guide
Land Art In the UK
Land Art in Close-Up
Land Art In the U.S.A.
Land Art: Pocket Guide
Installation Art in Close-Up
Minimal Art and Artists In the 1960s and After
Colourfield Painting
Land Art DVD, TV documentary
Andy Goldsworthy DVD, TV documentary
The Erotic Object: Sexuality in Sculpture From Prehistory to the Present Day
Sex in Art: Pornography and Pleasure in Painting and Sculpture
Postwar Art
Sacred Gardens: The Garden in Myth, Religion and Art
Glorification: Religious Abstraction in Renaissance and 20th Century Art
Early Netherlandish Painting
Leonardo da Vinci
Piero della Francesca
Giovanni Bellini
Fra Angelico: Art and Religion in the Renaissance
Mark Rothko: The Art of Transcendence
Frank Stella: American Abstract Artist
Jasper Johns
Brice Marden
Alison Wilding: The Embrace of Sculpture
Vincent van Gogh: Visionary Landscapes
Eric Gill: Nuptials of God
Constantin Brancusi: Sculpting the Essence of Things
Max Beckmann
Caravaggio
Gustave Moreau
Egon Schiele: Sex and Death In Purple Stockings
Delizioso Fotografico Fervore: Works In Process 1
Sacro Cuore: Works In Process 2
The Light Eternal: J.M.W. Turner
The Madonna Glorified: Karen Arthurs

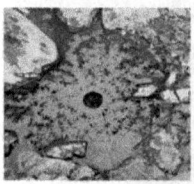

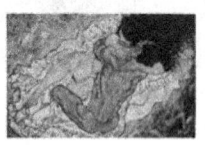

LITERATURE

J.R.R. Tolkien: The Books, The Films, The Whole Cultural Phenomenon
J.R.R. Tolkien: Pocket Guide
Tolkien's Heroic Quest
The *Earthsea* Books of Ursula Le Guin
Beauties, Beasts and Enchantment: Classic French Fairy Tales
German Popular Stories by the Brothers Grimm
Philip Pullman and *His Dark Materials*
Sexing Hardy: Thomas Hardy and Feminism
Thomas Hardy's *Tess of the d'Urbervilles*
Thomas Hardy's *Jude the Obscure*
Thomas Hardy: The Tragic Novels
Love and Tragedy: Thomas Hardy
The Poetry of Landscape in Hardy
Wessex Revisited: Thomas Hardy and John Cowper Powys
Wolfgang Iser: Essays and Interviews
Petrarch, Dante and the Troubadours
Maurice Sendak and the Art of Children's Book Illustration
Andrea Dworkin
Cixous, Irigaray, Kristeva: The *Jouissance* of French Feminism
Julia Kristeva: Art, Love, Melancholy, Philosophy, Semiotics and Psychoanalysis
Hélene Cixous I Love You: The *Jouissance* of Writing
Luce Irigaray: Lips, Kissing, and the Politics of Sexual Difference
Peter Redgrove: Here Comes the Flood
Peter Redgrove: Sex-Magic-Poetry-Cornwall
Lawrence Durrell: Between Love and Death, East and West
Love, Culture & Poetry: Lawrence Durrell
Cavafy: Anatomy of a Soul
German Romantic Poetry: Goethe, Novalis, Heine, Hölderlin
Feminism and Shakespeare
Shakespeare: Love, Poetry & Magic
The Passion of D.H. Lawrence
D.H. Lawrence: Symbolic Landscapes
D.H. Lawrence: Infinite Sensual Violence
Rimbaud: Arthur Rimbaud and the Magic of Poetry
The Ecstasies of John Cowper Powys
Sensualism and Mythology: The Wessex Novels of John Cowper Powys
Amorous Life: John Cowper Powys and the Manifestation of Affectivity (H.W. Fawkner)
Postmodern Powys: New Essays on John Cowper Powys (Joe Boulter)
Rethinking Powys: Critical Essays on John Cowper Powys
Paul Bowles & Bernardo Bertolucci
Rainer Maria Rilke
Joseph Conrad: *Heart of Darkness*
In the Dim Void: Samuel Beckett
Samuel Beckett Goes into the Silence
André Gide: Fiction and Fervour
Jackie Collins and the Blockbuster Novel
Blinded By Her Light: The Love-Poetry of Robert Graves
The Passion of Colours: Travels In Mediterranean Lands
Poetic Forms

POETRY

Ursula Le Guin: Walking In Cornwall
Peter Redgrove: Here Comes The Flood
Peter Redgrove: Sex-Magic-Poetry-Cornwall
Dante: Selections From the Vita Nuova
Petrarch, Dante and the Troubadours
William Shakespeare: Sonnets
William Shakespeare: Complete Poems
Blinded By Her Light: The Love-Poetry of Robert Graves
Emily Dickinson: Selected Poems
Emily Brontë: Poems
Thomas Hardy: Selected Poems
Percy Bysshe Shelley: Poems
John Keats: Selected Poems
Joh n Keats: Poems of 1820
D.H. Lawrence: Selected Poems
Edmund Spenser: Poems
Edmund Spenser: Amoretti
John Donne: Poems
Henry Vaughan: Poems
Sir Thomas Wyatt: Poems
Robert Herrick: Selected Poems
Rilke: Space, Essence and Angels in the Poetry of Rainer Maria Rilke
Rainer Maria Rilke: Selected Poems
Friedrich Hölderlin: Selected Poems
Arseny Tarkovsky: Selected Poems
Arthur Rimbaud: Selected Poems
Arthur Rimbaud: A Season in Hell
Arthur Rimbaud and the Magic of Poetry
Novalis: Hymns To the Night
German Romantic Poetry
Paul Verlaine: Selected Poems
Elizaethan Sonnet Cycles
D.J. Enright: By-Blows
Jeremy Reed: Brigitte's Blue Heart
Jeremy Reed: Claudia Schiffer's Red Shoes
Gorgeous Little Orpheus
Radiance: New Poems
Crescent Moon Book of Nature Poetry
Crescent Moon Book of Love Poetry
Crescent Moon Book of Mystical Poetry
Crescent Moon Book of Elizabethan Love Poetry
Crescent Moon Book of Metaphysical Poetry
Crescent Moon Book of Romantic Poetry
Pagan America: New American Poetry

MEDIA, CINEMA, FEMINISM and CULTURAL STUDIES

J.R.R. Tolkien: The Books, The Films, The Whole Cultural Phenomenon
J.R.R. Tolkien: Pocket Guide
The *Lord of the Rings* Movies: Pocket Guide
The Cinema of Hayao Miyazaki
Hayao Miyazaki: *Princess Mononoke*: Pocket Movie Guide
Hayao Miyazaki: *Spirited Away*: Pocket Movie Guide
Tim Burton : Hallowe'en For Hollywood
Ken Russell
Ken Russell: *Tommy*: Pocket Movie Guide
The Ghost Dance: The Origins of Religion
The Peyote Cult
Cixous, Irigaray, Kristeva: The *Jouissance* of French Feminism
Julia Kristeva: Art, Love, Melancholy, Philosophy, Semiotics and Psychoanalysis
Luce Irigaray: Lips, Kissing, and the Politics of Sexual Difference
Hélene Cixous I Love You: The *Jouissance* of Writing
Andrea Dworkin
'Cosmo Woman': The World of Women's Magazines
Women in Pop Music
HomeGround: The Kate Bush Anthology
Discovering the Goddess (Geoffrey Ashe)
The Poetry of Cinema
The Sacred Cinema of Andrei Tarkovsky
Andrei Tarkovsky: Pocket Guide
Andrei Tarkovsky: *Mirror*: Pocket Movie Guide
Andrei Tarkovsky: *The Sacrifice*: Pocket Movie Guide
Walerian Borowczyk: Cinema of Erotic Dreams
Jean-Luc Godard: The Passion of Cinema
Jean-Luc Godard: *Hail Mary*: Pocket Movie Guide
Jean-Luc Godard: *Contempt*: Pocket Movie Guide
Jean-Luc Godard: *Pierrot le Fou*: Pocket Movie Guide
John Hughes and Eighties Cinema
Ferris Bueller's Day Off: Pocket Movie Guide
Jean-Luc Godard: Pocket Guide
The Cinema of Richard Linklater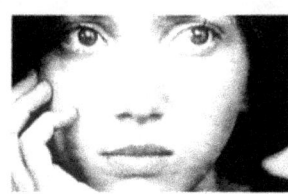
Liv Tyler: Star In Ascendance
Blade Runner and the Films of Philip K. Dick
Paul Bowles and Bernardo Bertolucci
Media Hell: Radio, TV and the Press
An Open Letter to the BBC
Detonation Britain: Nuclear War in the UK
Feminism and Shakespeare
Wild Zones: Pornography, Art and Feminism
Sex in Art: Pornography and Pleasure in Painting and Sculpture
Sexing Hardy: Thomas Hardy and Feminism

The Light Eternal is a model monograph, an exemplary job. The subject matter of the book is beautifully organised and dead on beam. (Lawrence Durrell)
It is amazing for me to see my work treated with such passion and respect. (Andrea Dworkin)

CRESCENT MOON PUBLISHING
P.O. Box 1312, Maidstone, Kent, ME14 5XU, Great Britain. www.crmoon.com

cresmopub@yahoo.co.uk   www.crescentmoon.org.uk

www.ingramcontent.com/pod-product-compliance
Lightning Source LLC
Chambersburg PA
CBHW062154080426
42734CB00010B/1679